FORTY

Dedication: To Dad

1924-2013

This collection of newspaper stories is dedicated to my father, Bill Kunerth, who taught journalism at Iowa State University for 30 years. In those years, he influenced the lives and careers of generations of journalists with his integrity, passion, and commitment to the truth. Known to many as "Wild Bill," he finished his distinguished career as an expert in public records and an advocate for the public's right to know.

He raised two journalists, myself and my brother Bill, who went on to have a successful career as a newspaper publisher. I spent my life as newspaper reporter with the Orlando Sentinel. This book owes its existence to 40 years of my father's nagging: you ought to pull your stories together and put them in a book.

See Dad, I listen to you.

About this book

I was privileged in my four decades at the Orlando Sentinel that the paper gave me the opportunity to write good stories. This came with the blessing of good editors who gave me encouragement and good assignments. They provided me the forum and format for exploring the people, places, events and issues of our time.

In this book you'll find Faces in the Crowd, a day-in-the-life approach to write broadly about demographics; Faces and Places, a series that went in search of a sense of place in Central Florida; Facing the Future, a continuing series of predicting the future which can make you pretty stupid in retrospect but I think I got Time right; Knock On Any Door, my attempt to prove everybody has a story; Kulture, a weekly column that was suppose to be about popular culture; On Any Given Sunday, a weekly feature of what people were doing on Sunday conceived as a caper to me get out of the office; It's Different Here, an occasional series that tried to explain this place to newcomers and old timers.

I've also included several projects or multi-day series: Old People, a special section on the myths and realities of aging: Barrier Breakers, a series on Orlando's first black police officers; Life Within

Limits, a series on an illiterate man; Anatomy of An Accident, a series on the effects of a car accident on six people.

The FAMU story, a narrative telling of the hazing death of drum major Robert Champion, was a contribution from myself and Denise Marie-Balona to the Sentinel's 2013 Pulitzer Prize finalist in Local Reporting.

Several of the stories are from my time as the paper's Atlanta bureau chief in the late 1980s and early '90s. Interspersed with those are times I was dispatched to write about events outside our circulation area. There's evidence here of my newspaperman's affinity for bars, bums and bank robbers.

In Living Memory stands apart as a meditative essay on memory and disaster published on the first anniversary of 9/11.

Everyone one of these stories, and there's more where those came from, represent a career in newspapers that went from manual typewriters to Twitter as a form of reporting. May you enjoy reading them as much as I loved writing them.

Jeff Kunerth

Published by Fifth Estate Media LLC, Maitland, FL
Nonfictionpublish.com

COVER DESIGN JESSE KUNERTH

FORTY

A modern history of Central Florida's places, culture, people and watershed moments as told through 40 years of journalism

JEFF KUNERTH

Contents

PEOPLE

A Big White Lie 10
A Life Within Limits: Gerald Hall 17
Faces In the Crowd: Jerry Tucker 29
Doll Baby 32
Bobby Johnson 35
Faces in the Crowd: Rusty and Charles 37
Faces in the Crowd: Susan Scora 40
Faces and Places: Maurices Market 44
Knock On Door: Six 47
Knock On Any Door: Flower Lady 50
Red Rountree: Bank Robber 53
Florida Governor Farris Bryant 58

PLACES

Running of the Chihuahuas 75
Faces and Places: Burton's Bar 77
Knock On Any Door: Poor 80
Flat tires, Fights, and Falstaffs 83
It's Different Here: Perfect Day 85
Old Store 87
One House: Mental Illness 90

AGE

Old People: Introduction 95
Old People: Muscle 98
Old People: Mind 105
Old People : Meaning. 112
Old People: Memory 119

CULTURE

On Any Given Sunday: Checker Kings 124
Orlando's First Black Police 126
Life Inside Extended Stay Motels 150
Faces in the Crowd: Illegal Immigration 161
Facing the Future: Time 165

WATERSHED

FAMU: A March to a Tragedy 175
Faces and Places: Disaster 185
Adam Walsh Slaying Puts City on Guard 190
Columbia Disaster: Heart of a Tragedy 196
Kimberly Mays: Switched at Birth 200
Georgia Cremation Scandal 202
Anatomy of an Accident 206
In Living Memory: A Year After 9/11 227

PEOPLE

A Big White Lie

Every family has its secrets. There are things parents never tell children. There are lies that become family legend. There are stories that were never meant to be told.

Judith Hartmann's secret, when she married Bill Myers in 1959, was that she was pregnant by a black man. When the baby born to two white parents came out black, the secret became a lie.

Throughout his childhood, David Myers was told that his skin color was a disease called melanism. He was lucky, his mother said, because the skin discoloration was all over his body, instead of just splotches of brown like most people had.

So despite his dark skin, Myers grew up in white, middle-class neighborhoods in Ohio and New York believing he was white.

"For many years I thought I was white. I thought like a white kid. There was a feeling in me that I didn't want to be associated with blacks. I wanted the story to be true," says Myers, a 45-year-old Orlando tennis teacher.

The secret shrouded in a lie lasted 26 years. Keeping it hidden all those years would turn Judy Myers into a hard, angry, unhappy woman, her family says. It made Dave Myers a defiant, rebellious, hostile child who would grow estranged from his parents, sisters and brother.

Learning the truth would send Myers on a search for identity. And it would convince him that his story is the story of America -- a white America that has been lied to, a black America oppressed and discriminated against, and a society unable or unwilling to discuss race.

When Judy Hartmann told Bill Myers that she was pregnant, he believed it was his.

And when the baby was born on Feb. 28, 1960 -- five months after their marriage -- he thought his son's skin color was jaundice. And then he thought there might have been a mix-up at the hospital.

And when his wife told him the doctors said it was a skin

disease that had turned their boy's skin dark, he thought she was telling the truth. No questions asked.

Because that is the kind of man Bill Myers is. He is soft and gentle and pliable, his children say. He accepts life as it comes, assumes the responsibilities of a man, a husband, a father.

As far as he was concerned, Dave Myers was as much his child as the three daughters and son who followed. If Judy said it was a skin disease, that was the end of the discussion.

"He never said a word," says Judy Myers, 67, who now lives with Bill in The Villages.

That attitude -- ignoring the obvious, believing the improbable -- filtered down to David and the other children. And in a family where everyone pretended that David was a darker shade of white, race was a taboo subject.

"There was no discussion. It never came up," says Bill Myers, 66, a retired welding engineer. "We hardly ever saw a black person."

The only blacks the Myerses saw in Stow, Ohio -- a white, middle-class town outside of Cleveland -- were in the papers or on the nightly news.

"That was the time of the ghettos," Bill says. "You read about the black ghetto on the east side of Cleveland, and the crime and the poor housing conditions."

When a young Dave Myers asked his mother why police in Alabama were spraying black civil-rights protesters with fire hoses, she told him it was because they were hot. Everything Myers saw growing up in Ohio and then the small town of Olean in western New York, convinced him it was better to be a white boy with a skin disease than a black kid.

"Why would I want to be black?" Myers says. "I saw how blacks were portrayed in the media."

As much as family members acted as though Dave was just like the other kids, they knew he wasn't. And the difference started showing up in his behavior. As Dave Myers entered adolescence, the trouble started. He became defiant, hostile and threatening. At one point, Myers was sent to live with a foster family. Another time, he was kicked out of the house and lived in his car.

"I was the black sheep of the family -- literally and figuratively," he says. "I was always in the doghouse or always getting out of the doghouse."

If Dave was treated differently, it was because of his behavior, not his skin color, his mother says.

"He was just uncontrollable. None of my other children acted this way," Judy says.

During those years, Judy Myers was an unhappy woman.

"She was a hard mother growing up," says Kathy Myers, 44. "Mom had a lot of anger inside her. She was tough, keeping all that inside."

The anger didn't end until, 26 years after David's birth, Judith Myers visited a psychiatrist who advised her to let go of the lie and tell her family the truth. What she told her husband and children was that she had been raped by a black man.

"I was not angry," Bill says. "I was glad that this load was released from her, and it answered a number of questions at the back of your mind that never seemed to be fully resolved."

With a new story, Judith Myers became a new person.

"I was much happier. I had a load off my back," Judy says. "I protected it well for many years."

David Myers was living in San Francisco at the time. He came home one night to find a message from his mother on his answering machine. On the message, she gave him the name of the black man who was his father -- Fermon Beckette Sr.

The way Fermon Beckette remembers it, there was no rape. He was working as an aide at a psychiatric ward in the same hospital where Judith Hartmann was a student studying nursing. She was 20. He was 10 years older. They went out a few times. The sex was consensual. No rape.

"That's an old fashioned, Southern lie," says Beckette, now a 77-year-old retired steel mill worker. "Knowing the situation, I can see how she would deny it. After all, she had to hide it to save her marriage."

Judy Myers insists the rape story is true: "Any black who rapes a woman will say she asked for it."

But if shedding the skin-disease story liberated Judith Myers, it plunged David Myers into an identity crisis.

"When my mother told me the truth, I went through a period of being homeless -- three years," he says.

He was a black man who knew nothing about being black. His family wasn't black. None of his neighbors had been black. None of his classmates had been black. Few of his friends were black.

Myers embarked on a self-education about all the things he never learned about black history, black culture, and race relations.

He has 10 spiral notebooks filled with notes he has taken from the books he has read such as The Destruction of Black Culture, Theories of Race and Racism, The Illusion of Integration and the Reality of Race, Growing Up in a Divided Society, and Lies My Teacher Told Me.

And then he set out to meet his black family members. He found a half-brother in Cleveland who led him to his black father. They talked on the phone, exchanged photographs.

On June 22, Dave Myers met Fermon Beckette Sr. for the first time.

"He struck me as trying to be a journalist, like he was researching a story, a project," Beckette says. "He sounded like he was in search of his identity."

Beckette feels some sympathy for the son he fathered, but never knew. "If you don't know what color you are in this country," he says, "you are headed for a lot of problems."

At different times in his life, Dave Myers has checked the box for white, the box for black, the box for other. Friends told him he was the whitest black guy they knew: He dressed white, he talked white. So for a time, Dave Myers tried to trade his Midwestern Ohio accent for a Southern black dialect, only to realize how dishonest it sounded coming from his mouth.

"It was a complete phoniness to me," he says.

After years of trying on different identities, Myers now believes he knows who he is and what he needs to do. He is the product of a black man and a white woman who must tell his story -- and his family's secrets -- so that blacks and whites can better understand each other.

"I hope that people can learn from my experience," he says.

So Myers has started his own Web site -- discuss race.com -- that features "The Dave Myers Story" and a list of books he has read.

But in his attempts to enlighten the greater society about the lies, secrets and deceptions of race in America, Myers often comes across as lecturing or chiding those he is trying to persuade, says Pete Lorins, a Haitian-born acquaintance who helped Myers with his Web site.

"I believe you cannot reach a good dialogue on race by telling people what they did wrong," Lorins says.

And it is that approach that has led to Dave being disowned by his family. His parents and sister complain that they cannot have a normal relationship with Myers. Every family gathering, every conversation, leads to a past they have no interest in reliving. He wants them to face the truth; they want to eat chicken supper without guilt.

"He always has to get into racial discussions or the `poor me' discussions," says Bill Myers. "He can't accept the way things are and go forward with his life. He has to keep stirring up the dirty water."

Dave's contention that racism is responsible for the problems in his life, his mother says, has made her more prejudiced against blacks.

"He has with his actions totally soured me on the black race," she says.

Dave and his mother haven't spoken for two years -- not since he appeared on a cable TV program and told everybody the skin-disease story. And now, as the story spreads to the Internet and the pages of the Orlando Sentinel, Judy Myers says she is ready to take his picture off the hallway wall and throw it in the trash.

"He's not my child," she says. "He's not a part of our lives anymore."

***

Dave Myers stands alone in the community room of the Southwest Public Library in the Dr. Phillips area with his three tables of books on race.

Dressed in a white shirt, tie, striped suspenders and dark slacks,

Myers leans against a table, waiting for the crowd to arrive.

For weeks, he posted fliers on "The Race Myth . . . debunked." The fliers identify him as "Dave Myers -- Subject Matter Expert" and direct people to his Web site.

But nearly two hours after the doors open at 10 a.m., nobody has arrived. Even the person he hired to set up audiovisual equipment hasn't shown up. The lull gives Myers time to think about what he might say, what myths he might debunk, if anybody attends. There is so much that white America needs to know. So much that Southern blacks need to hear. But where to start, what to say, he hasn't quite decided.

"You have to play it by ear. It's like stand-up. It's contingent on what the crowd gives you," he says.

As the clock approaches noon, a middle-aged white woman wanders in, followed by her elderly mother.

"What are you doing here?" the woman asks.

"Well, I'm discussing some of the books I've read," he says. "It's really about what is going on in the United States. We have a race issue."

"I had a little black girlfriend when I was 6 and she was 6," the woman volunteers.

"Do you have any black friends now?" Myers asks.

"I don't have any friends at all," the woman says.

"I don't either," Myers says. "That doesn't matter much."

He is midway through a history lesson on W.E.B. DuBois that has morphed into a discussion about the Nile River, when the woman interrupts him.

"My son married a black girl and they have two beautiful children," she says.

"Well," responds Myers, "I think mulatto children are the wave of the future."

The woman's remark gives Myers the opening he needs to tell the two women his life story. When he gets to the part about being raised to believe that his skin color was the result of a disease, the ladies giggle.

"Have you ever met your father?" the mother asks.

"Yes, I did, just a couple of months ago," he says.

"And was he nice?"

"Oh, yes, he was very nice," Myers says.

"I'm glad you met your father," the daughter says.

Then they thank him and walk out the door. The two women are his only audience the whole day.

Myers believes the empty room proves how adverse Americans are to talking about race -- its myths, its secrets, its lies: "The naked topic scares people away."

Disappointed but undaunted, Myers still envisions the day when his story -- the story of his family secret, the story of race in America -- will reach a wider audience.

In finding himself, Dave Myers fantasizes that someday he will find himself on Oprah.

September 18, 2005

A Life Within Limits: Gerald Hall

Every life has its accidents and tragedies, turning points and disappointments. For some, these are mere setbacks, challenges to be attacked and defeated before moving on. For others, they are catastrophic events that are so big, so immense, they define everything else to come.

When Gerald Hall looks back on the trajectory of his life, he recognizes the moment when everything changed. That day was 58 years ago. An instant of childhood exuberance took his world of possibilities and limited it to a few people, a few interests, a few miles from home. That moment limited the way Hall could look at the world and what the world saw when it looked back.

It explains why Gerald Hall rides an 18-speed bicycle but never changes gears. On this morning, Hall props open the laundry room door of his Orlando home and carries his bicycle outside. He will ride the blue Cignal Cherokee bike three miles to the Orlando Public Library through a visual blizzard of verbiage. Words on businesses. Words on signs. Words planted on wooden spikes stuck in front yards. Words taped to telephone poles. Words painted on the sides of trucks.

Along the way, he recites the words he recognizes, ignores the rest.

"Keep out. One way. Speed limit 30," says Hall, 63. "No parking. Downtown. Orange Avenue. State trooper."

He can't read the sign that says "Wadeview Park," or "coming soon" or "Florida residents." He knows the route to the library and back, has ridden it dozens of times, but can't give directions.

He also can't read a map or comprehend a bus schedule. Illiteracy keeps him from filling out an employment application or using a phone book. When he goes grocery shopping, his list is only as long as he can keep in his head and haul in the fold-out baskets on the back of his bicycle.

He has never driven a car. Never read a book or written a letter. Never made a true friend or fallen in love.

To him, words are like people. They aren't always as they

appear. They confuse and deceive.

"Some words look like what they say and some words don't," he says. "You say `for sale,' but it looks like `sa-lee.' It should be `Peps-I,' but you say `Pep-see.' That's when it gets confusing."

To decipher the words on a page, he needs someone he can trust. For much of his life, his mother, Grace Hall, was that person. But she died in 1977. Then it was his older brother Earl Hall, until he died in 1994. After that, there were some nieces and a couple of neighbors, but they all moved or passed away.

Hall's dependency upon others strains those relationships. He seldom speaks with his sister in Pennsylvania, is estranged from his brother in Oregon, and has an off-and-on friendship with a neighbor he relied upon to read for him.

Even his financial guardian has recoiled from becoming too involved in Hall's life.

"I was feeling that he was perceiving me as his mother, filling in that void where she left off," says Jenny Shuff-Dowd, director of Seniors First guardianship program.

Uncomfortable in crowds, self-conscious around others, Hall lives in self-imposed exile.

"My sister says I'm too by myself. I need to be around people more," Hall says. "But she didn't get hit by a car or anything. She went to a regular school. She didn't grow up like I did."

To those he confides in, Hall explains his illiteracy as a learning disability that resulted from an accident when he was a child.

"If it hadn't been for the accident, I would have been smart," says Hall. "That's what they always told me."

***

The ambulance had curtains on the windows.

That is all he remembers of the day in 1946 when he ran into the street and was struck by a car.

Gerald Hall's parents had just moved into the Franklin Terrace public-housing project in Erie, Pa. His father was working for the railroad as a pipefitter. His older brothers, Robert, Earl and Fred, had all moved out of the house. Another, Jack, died in infancy. His brother Paul, born with severe retardation, was in a state institution.

At home, it was just Gerald, his sister, Joan, and his parents in the three-bedroom apartment. The projects were new then. Everybody was white. Most every kid had two parents.

At 6, Joan was a year older than Gerald, who was the last of Grace Hall's seven children. Joan was taking Gerald to see their mother at Ricardo's Restaurant on East Lake Road.

The restaurant was six blocks from their apartment. Brother and sister walked together until they got to East Lake, a busy, two-lane avenue with a grassy median separating the traffic. At the curb, across from the restaurant, Gerald ran into the street.

"He didn't make it to the median," recalls Joan Hall Curry.

As the family tells the story, it was a Cadillac that hit Gerald, sending him into the air, his head striking the hood ornament above his temple and below the hairline. Gerald was taken to St. Vincent's Hospital where, 20 years later, Joan would study nursing. Nobody remembers how long Gerald was hospitalized. Nobody remembers him coming home.

All Gerald Hall knows about that day came from his mother's retelling: how the doctors said the head injury was not severe; how there should be no permanent damage; how the driver of the car got Grace to sign a statement that it was not his fault; how Gerald's personality changed following the accident.

"My mother said I slowed down quite a bit. I went into a shell like," Hall says. "She said I wasn't as talkative."

Other children noticed too. Kids can smell weakness in another child. They called Gerald dummy, stupid, retard. The adults weren't much better.

"When anyone new moved in, they'd tell 'em, `Watch out for that Hall kid. He's a half-wit. He's not right in the head.' Oh, it was terrible," he says.

The only time Hall felt safe was when he was with his mother. After the accident, Grace and Gerald were seldom separated. They lived together -- mother caring for son, son caring for mother -- until Grace Hall died at age 81.

"I was always around my mother. All my life you might as well say. Just about," says Hall, whose father died in 1955.

To his brothers and sister, Grace Hall seemed overprotective and indulgent of Gerald. She became his mother hen, he became her momma's boy. What Gerald wanted, Gerald got. What Gerald didn't want to do, Gerald didn't have to.

"She coddled him," Joan Curry says. "That was the way for her to acknowledge her guilt -- `I shouldn't have been in that restaurant and now I have to make up for it.' Today, we know that doesn't work."

August 22, 2004

Pages of Borrowed Memories

There is one small clothes closet in Gerald Hall's house. Inside the closet are three jackets, a couple of sweaters, jeans, a sport coat still sheathed in plastic, socks folded and placed on top of his shoes.

And a large stack of high-school yearbooks.

Hall started collecting yearbooks in 1989, beginning with Winter Park High School. Three months later, he bought the high-school yearbook from Port Allegheny, Pa., his father's hometown. During the next three years, he bought 11 more yearbooks, including ones for Edgewater, Boone, Oak Ridge and Colonial. The last yearbook he bought in 1993 was from Wilson Middle School in Erie, where he went to school.

Hall can't explain his fascination with the yearbooks of schools he never attended, students he never knew and words he can't read. But there is something he sees inside those books that reminds him of his own past, the childhood he had, the life he missed out on.

A year after the accident, Hall entered first grade at Wayne Elementary in Erie, Pa. He was given two intelligence tests that measured his IQ in the 70s. A person with an IQ in the range of 69 to 84 has a low intelligence but is not retarded. With an IQ in the 70s, most people should be able to read up to about the sixth-grade level.

Gerald never did. He was placed in special-education classes for those with learning disabilities. Through 10 years of school, he never progressed beyond the third-grade level.

“In the special classes, if you caught on, well all right, and if you didn't, you didn't," he says. "I guess it was your problem if you didn't learn."

At Academy High School in Erie, the special-ed classroom was in the basement, across from the wood shop and next to the boiler room. The only windows were along the top of the wall, level with the ground outside. They were made of frosted glass and never open.

Mrs. Crane, the teacher, sat at the front of the room, facing a dozen students. One boy, seated in the front row, stood out. Jimmy was his name. Gerald envied Jimmy. Jimmy was blond. Jimmy was tall. Jimmy could read.

"I don't know why he was in our class," Gerald says. "He didn't seem like he fit in there."

Mrs. Crane would have Jimmy stand in the front of the class and read stories. Gerald sat in the middle of the classroom, surrounded by the other kids, the special kids, the slow kids, the dummies, and watched Jimmy read. And when he looked at Mrs. Crane, he saw an expression on her face that was never there when a teacher looked at him.

"She would smile when Jimmy read," Hall says.

Hall tried to drop out of school, but instead was sent to the Gertrude Barber Exceptional Children Center where, beside the trainable retarded, he made pine-cone Christmas wreaths and phone book covers. He refinished furniture and sorted screws by size.

When he looks at the pictures inside the yearbooks, Gerald Hall sees everything that high school is, but was not for him. The football games, the dances, the smiles, the mugging for the camera. Everybody is happy inside the covers of a high-school yearbook. It's all a fraud, of course. But to Hall, it looks like the alternative universe of his life -- if a car hadn't hit him, if he had grown up normal, instead of special.

"Everybody looks happy," he says. "Making faces. They're all having fun. It's the best time of your life, I guess you could call it."

The one thing Gerald Hall did learn in school was reinforced by his mother at home: When the going gets tough, it's time to stop trying.

"It's always easier to quit," Hall says. "And I do."

His mother, as doting as she was, never worked with Gerald at home on his school lessons, never urged him to try harder, never pushed him to succeed, never asked him what he wanted to be when he grew up, never encouraged him to find a job, learn a trade, fall in love.

Gerald was her boy who never grew up, who never left home. He was the caterpillar who went into his cocoon and came out still a caterpillar.

August 23, 2004

Protected from the World Until Left to Face it Alone

Gerald Hall has only worked two jobs in his life. The first was in the kitchen of the Hamot Hospital in Erie, Pa. -- a job obtained for him by the Gertrude Barber Exceptional Children Center when he was in his early 20s. The work involved washing out large pots and pans in the steam and heat of the hospital kitchen.

Gerald lasted six months.

"I'd rather be a janitor than be in that kitchen," he says. "My mother said if you don't like it, then don't do it."

Grace Hall never urged her son to find another job, content to have Gerald at home, where he tended the family garden and his uncle's rose bushes.

Hall's illiteracy was always a stumbling block, an inhibitor, when he thought about looking for work. A job application was like someone speaking to him in a foreign language. A lot of jobs required the ability to read. Some employers want you to have a high-school diploma. It wasn't worth the embarrassment, the everyday reminder of his failures in school.

It was easier to stay home with Mom.

But the protective shell Hall lived inside was shattered

the day his mother died. Grace Hall had been in poor health since she sold their house in Erie and moved with Gerald to Orlando in 1972 to be near her second-oldest son, Earl. She rarely left her easy chair in the small living room where she spent her days watching television.

Mother and son were watching soap operas on June 5, 1977, eating TV dinners Gerald had made for lunch. Excusing herself, Grace got up from her chair and went into the bathroom at the back of the house.

Minutes passed, and she didn't come back. Gerald went to see if his mother was all right. In the kitchen, Hall could hear his mother gasping for air from behind the bathroom door.

He pushed open the door. His mother was slumped face first on the floor. Her head had hit the edge of the shower stall and her glasses had cut her above the eye. Blood leaked onto the linoleum floor. Gerald knelt beside his mother's body and patted her gently on the back.

"Mom?" he said.

She didn't respond. He knew she was dead and his life would never recover.

Hall called Earl, who called an ambulance. Before the paramedics arrived, Hall covered his mother with a sheet.

Dead of a heart attack, Grace Hall was cremated and her ashes returned to Erie. For her funeral service in Orlando, Hall's oldest brother, Robert, flew in from California and his sister, Joan, came in from Erie. Four friends of Earl came, but none of Grace Hall's neighbors attended the funeral.

At 37, Gerald was alone for the first time in his life.

His mother's death sent Hall into a depression that never completely went away. For the past few years, he has been taking anti-depressant medications. At the time, his family felt a job would be a cure for his blues and a step toward self-sufficiency. A niece was dating a builder who hired Gerald to clean up his construction sites.

Gerald Hall was working a steady job for the first time in his life, making $50 a week.

"I liked it. It made me feel good," he says. "He went out of business or I might be working with him today."

The job lasted three years, but when it ended, so did Gerald Hall's working career. Others would encourage him to get a job, but he never did.

Instead, Hall lives on less than $600 a month from his father's railroad pension and veterans benefits.

Yet there are times, at night, when a different life, a productive life with purpose, seems almost within reach.

"I had a crazy dream last night. I dreamed I got off all my medications and I was all right. And then I went out and got a job. I was in a store, a grocery store, putting things on the shelf. And then it ended," he says. "It was a good dream, I thought."

August 24, 2004

Friendships Wilt in One-Way Relationships

The morning sky is the color of eggshell. The air is cool, the grass is still wet with dew as Gerald Hall clips the leash to his dog's collar. Hall is wearing one of his two favorite shirts, the Run Around the Pines T-shirt given to him by Seniors First.

Hall is 6 feet tall, 180 pounds. The scar from his childhood accident blends in with the lines of his face, a faint upside-down J on the left side of his forehead.

When he walks, it's with his head down, shoulders hunched as if giving the world a piggyback ride.

As they walk, Precious tugging hard at the leash, Gerald points out the homes of neighborhood pets: Nola the pig, Baby the Chihuahua, Rocky the Dalmatian.

But when they reach the corner of Simonton and Ontario avenues, Hall lowers his head, averts his eyes from the house on the corner, and pulls Precious in the opposite direction.

Bob Wollnick lives inside the small brown house with peeling paint that sits far back from the street behind an elaborate garden. Wollnick, a 71-year-old widower, met Hall about two years ago as Gerald was walking his dog.

The men became friends. Wollnick gave Hall a jacket from Universal Studios, invited him over to eat, lent him money. Hall came to Wollnick whenever he had something that needed to be read.

"Every time he had a piece of paper, he came running to the house," Wollnick says. "Basically, he has no friends as far as I know."

Like many who have met Hall, Wollnick saw a person trapped in routine, self-conscious and shy, afraid to try something new and different, always low on money. He also recognized Hall as someone with a mind that absorbs whatever he is told and a determination that is its own form of intelligence.

"He's not retarded," Wollnick says. "He remembers everything. He's very smart to a point."

Wollnick showed Hall where he could buy day-old bread, tried to get Gerald to go to the flea markets with him to save money and urged him to get a job at a business that hires the handicapped. Hall would have none of it.

"He doesn't want to take advice from people. He's very independent that way," Wollnick says.

When Wollnick, who likes to take vacations overseas, asked Hall to mow his lawn while he was gone, Gerald refused. Later, when Hall was three months late repaying money he borrowed from Wollnick, the friendship was over.

"The reason I ended the relationship is it was a one-way street. I don't need you as a friend, I told him. Flat dropped him," Wollnick says.

Hall refuses to refer to Wollnick by name -- calling him "that man" with a dismissive wave of his hand. But the loss of the friendship confuses and hurts Hall, who clings to those who befriend him like a drowning man to the side of a lifeboat.

"I might have shattered his daydream when I told him I didn't want to be his friend anymore. Maybe that's not the right thing to do," Wollnick says. "I didn't want to be his caregiver."

The falling out with Wollnick was a repeat of Hall's estrangement with his older brother, Robert Hall, who lives in Oregon. The brothers have not spoken since Gerald asked to borrow money six years ago.

"He used to call me and I'd call his wife," Hall says. "Then he got mad when I asked for the $100. He said, `I'm no bank.' `Gee,' I said, `I'm no stranger. I'm your brother,' I said. He said, `Don't call me. I'll call you.' But he never did call me."

Needy, yet selfish, Gerald Hall has never had a true friendship in his life. It baffles him when his relationships dissolve.

"Everybody's stopped talking to me. I don't know why," he says. "What did I say?"

August 26, 2004

His Special Day is Wrapped in Waiting

The defining day of Gerald Hall's life was 58 years ago when he gave into the impulsive urge to run across the street.

One other day remains special, one day out of 365: his birthday. He looks forward to that day like a child waits for Christmas.

His birthdays are not filled with friends, family, cake and candles. No presents wrapped in colorful paper and decorated with ribbons and bows.

They are spent, like his other days, alone. But they always begin with the expectation that the day will end with a card in the mailbox or a phone call from his sister.

On the day he turns 63, Hall awakens optimistic.

"I might get a birthday card today," he says after his breakfast of plain toast and tea.

He is hoping it will be a talking card such as the one his sister Joan sent last time. He saves his birthday cards, like everything else he values. The last one he received from his brother Robert arrived on his 57th birthday and plays the Happy Birthday song when you open it.

Joan's card makes laughing sounds when you open it. It's the laughing he likes. The words are a mystery.

He decides on his birthday to make another trip to the Washington Mutual branch bank building being torn down on Curry Ford Road. He's been watching the building come down off and on all week long. When he pulls up on his bike, a female construction worker gives him the thumbs-up sign of recognition.

The sky is as flawless as a wall waiting to be painted. Cars rush by with people on the way to work or back home, all too busy with something else to stand for an hour to watch an old building come apart. The heavy machinery groans and clanks. A bulldozer pushing around the debris backs up: beep beep beep beep.

The morning is starting to heat up. Taking off his helmet, Gerald Hall runs his hand over the top of his head. His haircut is the same as when he was 9. He watches the machinery with a right hand on his hip, his camera dangling by its strap from his left wrist.

"Maybe I ought to snap a few pictures," he says.

Back home, he checks his answering machine, thinking maybe Joan might have called while he was gone.

"No, it isn't blinking," he says. "So she didn't call."

Hall is accustomed to spending his birthdays alone. But he tries to make the day special in his own way, treating himself to a meal at Brian's Restaurant -- a five-mile bike ride from his home. He has been going to Brian's on his birthday for the past few years, ever since someone at Seniors First said you could get a good home-style meal for a reasonable price.

The first time at Brian's, Hall was dismayed when he opened the menu to find it was all words. No pictures like the Steak 'n Shake menu.

"I told the waitress I can't read and asked her what's on the menu. She said the grouper is good," he says.

Since then he always orders the grouper meal. On his birthday, he gets the fried grouper, beef-pepper-and-rice soup, sweet peas, mashed potatoes, unsweetened iced tea and a slice of cherry pie with a scoop of vanilla ice cream on top.

The bill comes to $12.35, an exorbitant price for a man who hates spending money on food.

Back home from his lunch, Hall checks the mailbox. Inside is only a card soliciting donations for the Orlando Union Rescue Mission, addressed to "Caring Friend." He looks it over, and fails to recognize the word "friend." At 2:30 p.m the telephone rings and Hall jumps up.

"That might be my sister," he says.

He answers the phone: "Hello? Hello?" And hangs up, "Wrong number."

An hour later, he wonders aloud why he hasn't heard from his sister.

"I thought my sister would call already," he says. "She knows I usually go out to eat on my birthday. That's probably why she hasn't called."

Late in the afternoon, he checks the mailbox again. Maybe the card came special delivery. Maybe it was delivered to a neighbor's house by mistake.

Still nothing.

"It takes time. It comes from Sheffield, Pennsylvania. All depends on the flow of the mail," he says. "I'm not disappointed."

August 27, 2004

Faces in the Crowd: Jerry Tucker

They buried you near the crest of a hill in Highlands Memory Cemetery on Aug. 26, 1967. It was a beautiful, clear day, and the cemetery overflowed with people who came to mourn the first soldier from Apopka to die in Vietnam.

The marker on your grave is shiny gray-and-pink granite with a rust-colored name plate that says Jerry James Tucker was born on Sept. 17, 1946, and died on Aug. 19, 1967. A sniper's bullet killed you six weeks after you arrived in Vietnam.

Your mother visits the grave every couple of months. She'll be there today, Memorial Day, to replace the peach and pink silk roses that fade from the sun. She says roses and gladiolas remind her of you. She is 71 years old now. Her hair is long and silvery. Her face is heavily lined.

The year of your death, 9,463 Americans were killed in Vietnam. The next year it was 14,623. The war ended in 1975. Some say we lost, some say we quit. But when it was all over, 58,135 Americans had died.

We buried many of them - about one in four veterans - in the 115 national cemeteries where rows of identical headstones seem to go on forever like images reflected in two facing mirrors. The rest are sprinkled in graveyards across the country.

We've filled three national cemeteries in Florida with veterans and war casualties. Seven years ago they opened Florida National Cemetery in Bushnell and made it big enough to bury 4,000 veterans annually to beyond the year 2030.

For Memorial Day services, they line the entrance to the Bushnell cemetery with 500 flags that once draped the caskets of war's casualties.

Your mother kept her flag. She has it stored in a box along with all of your stuff on the top shelf of a bedroom closet. She framed your posthumous Purple Heart and Silver Star medals, and saved the 1967 Coca-Cola calendar you hung on your bedroom wall with the days marked off until Feb. 26, when you left for the Army.

She keeps the calendar in a black satchel. Inside the

satchel is also a little box with the contents of your wallet - phone numbers written on scraps of paper, directions to a house scribbled on a piece of green construction paper, a pocket-size 1966 State Bank of Apopka calendar, your draft card, fishing license, a copy of the Armed Forces code of conduct, and a $6 pay stub from the job you had, working for H.S. Musselwhite Jr. at his chicken farm.

It's the wallet of a man who never expected to die, who volunteered for the service right out of high school with every expectation of coming home. Guess you were no different from any of the 575,000 men and women who have lost their lives on the battlefield since the Revolutionary War.

You carried in your wallet a couple of black-and-white photos of Army buddies, one holding a rifle, the other leaving a latrine, and a bunch of pictures from high school classmates. Judy wrote on the back of hers: "To a real sweet-n-nice guy. I enjoyed your friendship these past years and hope to have your friendship always."

Diane, your girlfriend, returned your high school ring to your mother after your death. She married a guy who came back from the war, and they moved to Georgia.

Your brother Larry was 17 when you died. He'll be 46 in October. He quit the Apopka High School track team so he wouldn't break the record you set in the mile, and started getting into fights with kids at school who opposed the war. He dropped out and married Gayle. They've been together now for 27 years. Larry got his G.E.D. and has worked all his life installing and repairing air conditioners. He named the youngest of his two sons after you.

Your brother Terry, well, he broke up with his second wife and moved in with your folks. He has two kids and works as a groundskeeper. Terry still remembers how you left the imprint of your Future Farmers of America ring on the cheek of a bully.

Your sister Connie has been married twice, the second time for 12 years to Joe Davis, who drives a truck for Frito-Lay. They have two girls. Connie is 41 now and works in a school cafeteria. She framed a pencil rubbing of your name taken from the Vietnam War Memorial in Washington.

Diane, the sister you called "Button," was married for a couple of years, but she's single now and trying to adopt a child. She lives on 10 acres of land in Lake County with goats, chickens, cows and horses. Diane turned 40 in January and has worked for the same communications company for 22 years.

Your dad died in Georgia 20 years ago. He came to your funeral with his second wife and their two kids. Your mother, Vivian, and stepfather, Glenn, have been married for 42 years. Glenn retired in February from Palmer Electric after 33 years. He and your mom still live in the same house you grew up in on Aurora Drive, but you wouldn't recognize the place.

They changed the color from turquoise to brown, put a wooden wishing well on the front lawn where the big sycamore once stood. There's a flag pole in the front, too, and a lamppost smothered in jasmine.

You've been dead now eight years longer than you lived, but not a day goes by that your mother doesn't think of you. Her friends say she needs to let go and forget. They want her to throw away that black satchel and take down the pictures and mementos of you she has scattered throughout the house.

But Vivian, she's sentimental. She clings to your memory like she holds on to your possessions. Your absence occupies her like a hurt that will not heal. She saved all the souvenirs of your life, even the telegram from Major Gen. Kenneth E. Wickham, the one that began, "The Secretary of the Army has asked me to express his deepest regret. . . . "

Your mom was looking through that old satchel of your belongings the other day when she came upon a cardboard tube with a photograph inside she had never seen before. She unrolled the picture and found a group portrait of your basic training unit at Fort Benning, Ga. She searched for your face in the crowd of young uniformed men standing in rows like the stripes of a flag.

"All their faces look alike to me," she said.

Just like the tombstones of a military cemetery.

May 29, 1995

Doll Baby: A Story of Alzheimer's

She is an old woman in infancy. On her lap is a teddy bear, a child's toy belonging to a 95-year-old woman. Her body, its loose flesh hanging from fragile bones, is swathed in a baby's blanket of yellow, blue and pink stripes.

Her daughter calls her Doll Baby.

From her throat come small, cooing moans. Attempts at speech are stymied by the loss of words. It has been a long, long time since she has uttered her daughter's name. She may not remember it at all.

Rachel Clark married young, at 16, to a man nearly twice her age. To her daughter, Mrs. Clark remained forever a child, someone who never seemed to grow up even as she grew older.

"She liked to laugh. She liked to have fun," said her daughter, Shirley Margeson. "She liked all the things children like."

As a young woman, she always preferred to be called Ray instead of Rachel. She devoted her life to her four children, and when they grew up her 37-year marriage ended. After the divorce she waited for a fairy-tale ending that never came.

"She always thought a Prince Charming was going to take her off someplace. I think she kept this in her mind all the time," said Mrs. Margeson, who is in her 70s.

It wasn't until Alzheimer's disease began to eat away at her mind that Rachel Clark surrendered her childhood dreams, even as she began the process of becoming more childlike. As she stood in the doorway of her daughter's Winter Park home some years ago, having accepted the realization that her mind no longer functioned properly, Mrs. Clark conceded that her fantasy had ended.

Turning to her daughter, she said, "I always thought that I was somebody special."

Identified in 1906 by German neurologist Alois Alzheimer, Alzheimer's disease is an intellectual impairment that recent research has likened to the inverse of the maturation process. It is a disease that attacks the cerebral cortex of the brain, which contains a person's memory facilities.

As the irreversible, incurable disease progresses, the Alzheimer's victim undergoes what psychiatrist Barry Reisberg, director of the geriatric study and treatment program at New York University Medical Center, describes as essentially the opposite of childhood development.

The symptoms of Alzheimer's disease are mimicked by dozens of other infirmities, including malnutrition, drug intoxication, cardiovascular disease, brain trauma and pulmonary conditions. Currently, determining that a patient has Alzheimer's disease requires eliminating all other possibilities. There is no clinical test for Alzheimer's. The only sure way of diagnosing it is to perform an autopsy and look for telltale tangles of neurological fibers.

Reisberg hopes that through his studies of the disease's progress, physicians may be better able to determine whether a patient has Alzheimer's. A person's losing the ability to walk before becoming incontinent, for example, would indicate an illness other than Alzheimer's.

By the time many people have been diagnosed as having Alzheimer's, they have lost the ability to handle routine finances, plan a meal or go shopping. Soon they can no longer select the proper clothing.

When the disease becomes more advanced, the victims cannot put on their own clothes, bathe unaided or control their bodily functions. They have reverted to the stage of a 2-year-old child.

In the late stages of Alzheimer's, their vocabulary regresses from the five or six words that a 15-month-old child would have to the single word of a 12-month-old. From there, they lose the ability to walk or sit up. Then they forget how to smile.

Eventually their functions become limited, like a newborn baby's, to sucking and grasping.

"I never wanted any children," said Shirley Margeson. "Life is funny. I never had any."

Beneath the baby's blanket, Rachel Clark's hands shake. The old woman's wrists are bound to prevent her from picking at the bandage covering her right temple, where a patch of cancerous skin was removed. Her throat gurgles. She bends her head forward and touches her face with the softness of the blanket.

"I didn't like babies," said Mrs. Margeson. "My mother, she loved children. She kept giving me dolls and I didn't want them. I had a doll room, a room filled with dolls, but I never played with them."

Rachel Clark wears a diaper beneath her red slacks. Every morning her daughter lifts her out of bed and dresses her. In preparing her mother's meals, Mrs. Margeson reduces everything to baby-food consistency in a food processor. At night she undresses her mother, bathes her and lifts her back into bed.

"I didn't want any children because I couldn't stand the hurt," Mrs. Margeson said. "I hurt when somebody else hurts. Every time I think my mother hurts, I tell you, I feel terrible. I think I've died a thousand hurts, yet at the same time I wouldn't want to give any of them up because it means another day she's alive."

Outside, there is a motor home that has not left the driveway in four years.

"My whole life is caring for her. I mean 24 hours a day. I think she is entitled to it," Mrs. Margeson said. "She fed me, so I'm feeding her. How many times did she change my diaper?"

The recliner in which Mrs. Clark rests faces the door to the carport. Her sun-sensitive eyes are closed to the soft light that filters through plant leaves and cascades into the room. Behind their closed lids, her eyes are brown.

"To me, a mother is someone who takes care of you. You know what? I lost a mother. It was like she wasn't there anymore. You've lost that helping hand. Now you're the one. You have to turn it around," Mrs. Margeson said.

Long ago, Shirley Margeson stopped calling Rachel Clark "Mother."

"When I called her Mother, she was a different person," she said. "Now she's my Doll Baby."

October 6, 1985

Bobby Johnson: Can Collector

Bobby Johnson says he doesn't collect welfare. He collects aluminum cans. Makes a right good livin' off it, too.

"I make a livin' off 'em these cans. Before the night's over I get my wagon full, you better believe it. Yes sir," said Bobby. "I'm just tryin' to keep the city clean."

Bobby, a 59-year-old unemployed former factory worker, is one of three of four enterprising men scouring downtown Orlando for aluminum cans, pushing their shopping carts along the streets, behind restaurants, between alleys.

They sell the cans to scrap metal firms for 15 cents per pound.

"You can laugh at me if you want, but it's better 'an stealing," says Bobby.

His grey workman's hat has the brim pushed back. He wears tennis shoes, blue ones, and jeans with the cuffs turned up like a little boy's.

The people at the Orlando Iron and Mental Works, 1219 W. Robinson Street, know Bobby and his friends. Bobby has deocrated his shopping cart with an old bicycle license plate. Another of the can collectors, who sings a song every day to the recycling clerk, has American flags draped over his cart.

"I got a few bucks in my pocket,"Bobby boasts. "And you know why? I work. Oh, yeah. Made me a little money today."

Bobby says he makes $35 to $45 a week. Bobby exaggerates a little. Joe West, Metal Works owner, said the men make about $20 a week.

"You see them everywhere, pushing their carts. To these people that's a lot of money," West said. "It's a whole living for some of these guys."

Bobby has a crumpled pack of Winston Lights – one of the benefits to having money in your pocket – and he taps a cigarette from the pack into his bony fingers.

The bottle of wine passed between friends is another benefit.

"Heck, it's a living you know. It's better than nothing. You better believe it, yes sir. I rely on myself."

Across the street from one of Bobby's regular stops – a bar – is a parking lot. The parking lot attendant, a young muscular man in a white sleeveless T-shirt, laughs when he sees the picture of Bobby Johnson pushing his car along Court Street in the rain.

"Yeah, I know him. He's really a character. Every day he comes around here and collects cans from the bar across the street."

Sometimes Bobby and one of his fellow can collectors do odd jobs for the attendant. Sometimes they panhandle. But for the most part they push their custom shopping carts, looking for discarded aluminum cans before the garbage trucks can empty the hotel and restaurant dumpsters.

They have it down to a science. Each has a route and knows exactly when the garbage is set out, when the trucks come to empty the dumpster. Bobby said he figures he walks 35 miles a day looking for cans. His friends admit he's a storyteller.

"I walk 35 miles to get my load. I do sir. I ain't lying," Bobby says, his cigarette down to the filter. His hands are streaked with wrinkles. Dirt is embedded deep underneath his fingernails.

The highlight of his day, Bobby says, was when he stopped at the 7-Eleven store and found a gold mine of aluminum.

"Got me a whole load out there," he says with a toothless grin and begins to push his cart to the rear of the Angebilt Hotel. It's about time to fill the dumpsters.

August 19, 1975

Faces in the Crowd: Rusty & Charles

Rusty Hunt and Charles Johnson are walking up Orange Avenue. They have left their group home on Hillcrest Street, turned down Magnolia, cut across Concord, and are headed for Pine Street to catch Bus 22.

As he walks down the street, Charles Johnson waves at every car, greets every pedestrian. He has been warned against talking to strangers - and has yet to meet one: "How you doing, sir? Hey, buddy, how you doing? Hey, brother, God bless you. How you doing, ma'am?"

Johnson is a talker. Hunt is his echo.

"We've got a long way to walk," Johnson says.

"Long way to walk," says Hunt in a high-pitched squeaky voice that makes him sound more like a cartoon character than a 35-year-old man.

Johnson leads the way. He is a short, skinny guy with a long, large head, a blind left eye, and a bouncy gait.

Hunt waddles a step behind, a big, soft fellow with a walrus mustache and only one thing on his mind: the coffee shop.

The closer they get to the coffee shop, the faster Rusty Hunt walks. When he passes Johnson, his friend tries to reel him back: "Slow down, Russ. Heel, heel. Slow down, baby."

At intersections, they ignore the flashing orange hand and walk across with arms out, palms up, to slow the traffic.

When they reach the Traffic Stop Cafe, owner Joy Vera has two cups of coffee to go waiting for them on the counter.

"They've been coming here for as long as I've been open," Vera says. "They're never late."

The coffee shop is a landmark in their day, along with the hot dog stand where they stop after work for a can of Pepsi. For two men who cannot read, cannot write, cannot tell time, the day rolls through their lives as a series of guideposts anchored in the rock of routine.

It's 8 a.m. when it's time to leave the house; noon when it's time for lunch; 3 p.m. when it's time to go home from work.

Time is a slippery idea for Hunt and Johnson. Growing old doesn't worry them, because age doesn't mean anything.

Johnson believes he is 32.

Asked how old he is, Hunt's face darkens as he thinks. ''I'm 19,'' he decides.

''How long have I known you, Russ?'' Johnson asks.

''I don't know,'' replies Hunt.

''I don't know either,'' Johnson says. ''I think it's a year.''

They have known each other since the 1960s when they both lived in the Sunland center for the mentally retarded in Gainesville. Johnson lived there for 17 years from the age of 11. Hunt went in when he was 8 and came out when he was 20.

They moved into a group home together in the 1970s, when state mental institutions for all but the most severely disabled were closed.

Of the state Department of Health and Rehabilitative Services' 3,359 mentally retarded clients in Central Florida, only 288 are in institutional care. A small but growing number are living on their own. The majority live at home, the consequence of an HRS policy that leaves mentally retarded children with their families.

Johnson and Hunt have gone, in the course of their lives, from being ''inmates'' to ''patients'' to ''clients'' to ''consumers.'' The people who were once called idiots, morons, and feeble-minded are now known as the ''developmentally challenged.''

Hidden behind the obscure nomenclature of mental health is a change in the the thinking of the people who work with the mentally retarded. Whereas they were once defined by what they couldn't do, the mentally retarded are now grouped by what they can do. They are given choices, like other consumers, and challenges, like other adults.

''We don't know what they can do. They have never been given an opportunity,'' said Michele Levy, human-services program specialist with HRS' developmental services in Orlando.

Charles Johnson's grandest ambition is to live by himself.

''I could go anywhere, do anything, come home, take me a nap, watch TV,'' he says. ''I could go out to eat by myself, talk to people by myself. Talk to strangers.''

Rusty's goals are more modest: ''I'd like to go to the

movies. Eat popcorn, too. Nightclubs. I like to dance."

Johnson and Hunt have disproven the low expectations of their pediatricians. They have lived, and survived, on a level of understanding that values friendship, family, work and responsibility. They have worked together for 11 years at the Central Florida Sheltered Workshop, sorting coat hangers, making rags and tending plants in the nursery.

Their job for the day at the nursery is to sort and stack small mountains of plant trays that come, like people, in a variety of colors, shapes and sizes.

Unlike people, the broken trays are thrown away.

They get paid for their work, but they don't know how much.

"How much do we make, Russ?"

"I don't know."

"I don't know either."

Johnson and Hunt are naive about things other people find important, such as office politics, mortgage payments and retirement plans, but they are not the happy innocents portrayed in movies and fiction. They get depressed, frustrated, angry.

On the way back from work, Johnson displays his temper in a verbal sparring match with a woman on the bus.

"Just shut your mouth and leave me alone," he says. "Don't tell me what to do. You don't run my life. You think you're a know-it-all. I don't think so."

When the bus driver tells him to shut up, he sulks in his seat. On the walk back home from the bus station, Hunt and Johnson pass some police cars outside a parking garage.

"Somebody got caught here," Johnson says.

"Got caught," echoes Hunt.

Back at the group home, the residents sit in the living room and share the events of their day.

When it's his turn, Rusty Hunt stands up from his flower-print chair in the corner.

"I stacked trays up. Saw the police. I was in the lunch room and had a peanut butter and jelly sandwich. I had a Diet Coke," Hunt says, and then he smiles. "I had a good day."

July 11, 1994

Faces in the Crowd: Susan Scora

She looks at herself in the morning and sees That Look staring back in the mirror.

She was chubby all her life, a dark-haired, round-faced Italian girl growing up on Long Island. She started smoking in high school to lose weight, began drinking her coffee with artificial sweeteners during one of her innumerable diets.

Her face now is thin, cheekbones showing under the darkness beneath her brown eyes. It is one of the ironies of her life: The illness has made her pretty.

Hers is the temporal beauty of a flower before the frost.

"I'm afraid the disease is going to make me ugly," says Susan Scora. "I know it will. It's inevitable. I'm just not looking forward to it."

Scora has AIDS, one of 165 women in metropolitan Orlando with the disease. She belongs to one of the fastest-growing segments in the AIDS epidemic - women who contract the disease through heterosexual sex.

Last year, heterosexually transmitted AIDS increased three times faster among women than among men. More than a third of the 27,500 women who have contracted AIDS in the United States received it through heterosexual contact.

Scora has lost 35 pounds since being diagnosed in 1989. She eats now to gain weight, not lose it.

"Other people might not see it, but I know I have that look," says Scora, who weighs 130 pounds. "I'm gaunt, thin, drawn."

It is dark inside her apartment, the drapes pulled tight against the morning sun. Scora is dressed in a baggy, faded flannel shirt, gray sweat pants, white socks.

She awoke in the morning feeling like a car with the headlights left on overnight. The red warning light is on inside her head.

"I go with how I feel," she says. "Today is a day when I don't want to get dressed, I don't want to put my makeup on, I don't want to go anywhere."

In the last three years, she feels as if her body has turned old inside her: "It's like being very old very quickly. I'm a 36-year-old woman in an old person's body."

She tires easily. Her muscles always ache. Her stomach hurts. There's a sharp, intense pain in her side that doctors say is stress-related. She has a headache most of the time.

A rash on her skin won't go away. It makes her whole body itch. Three days a week she goes for sun-lamp treatments that assuage the itching with an ultraviolet salve.

Even when she doesn't itch, she tugs at her skin and rakes her face and arms with fingernails trimmed down to the quick.

"When I found out I had AIDS I had a mental breakdown. I just broke," she says, her voice raspy and thick with a New Yorker's accent. "I cried 24 hours a day. People used to give me a box of Kleenex as a gift - no joke."

She doesn't cry anymore. She went to 18 funerals in one year.

"We harden up because it happens so much," she says.

The rejection of friends and family that the doctor warned her about ("You have the leprosy of the '90s," he said) never came. Her family has been supportive; her friends have not withdrawn. But she senses the fear of AIDS that people carry inside them in the timidness of their handshakes and the recoiling of their embraces.

And she doesn't blame them.

"I don't want people to be scared of me, but I want them to be scared of the disease," Scora says. "There are people out there in the bars today who know it's not just a gay disease, who don't think it's going to happen to them. I find that to be so unbelievable. If I got it from a sexual encounter, it can happen to anyone."

She always thought her life would be a replay of her mother's: Meet a guy, get married, have kids. She wasn't a good student, never went to college. She got a job right out of high school and has worked as a waitress, a cashier, a customer-service representative, an assembly-line worker. She felt good in her self-sufficiency. But it was hard for her to meet men, and the ones she dated were all the wrong kind. She had fewer than 10 lovers in her life, her first when she was 17. One of the men - she doesn't know who - gave her AIDS. The final souvenir from a lifetime of bad men was a fatal disease.

"Not only did I have lousy relationships, now I'm going to die from it," she says.

The disease has changed her mind about men. Her closest friends are both men with AIDS; one a homosexual, the other an intravenous drug abuser. They have formed a triumvirate of friendship, the disease in their bodies curing some of the wounds of their psyches.

"We've bonded; we're best friends. We're going through this disease together," Scora says. "I don't equate men with hurt anymore."

Friendships are all she has now. Desire is still alive inside Susan Scora, but intimacy is something that belongs to her past.

"I'm not going to have the chance ever again to just lay in bed and have someone hold me in his arms," she says.

She lives with one of her male friends in a two-bedroom apartment decorated with donated furniture. Unable to work, she receives $536 a month in disability payments.

"You hate the fact you're on disability. You hate the fact you can't work," she says. "Work is basically what I did."

What she does now is talk. She talks to anyone who will listen about what it is like to have AIDS, how you get it, and how you avoid it. Her disease has given her life a significance she never knew before. A sense of purpose has replaced the feeling of failure.

"I used to think I wasn't a success. All those things I wanted in my life didn't happen," she says. "I asked God to allow this: Use me and don't let my life be useless."

A holiday Catholic most of her life, she has rediscovered religion. She believes in God, and miracles, and life everlasting. She has a crucifix in her bedroom draped with rosary beads.

Her apartment is decorated with her dried flower arrangements, a talent she discovered while bedridden last year. Fearing death was near, she made 30 wreaths as Christmas presents for friends and family.

"I wanted to leave everybody one thing that they could

have forever,'' she says.

In the afternoon, she sits at her kitchen table drinking coffee in a Santa Claus mug and chain-smoking Misty Menthol cigarettes. Outside her second-story window she can see children walking home from school. She hears their giggles and loud voices.

Scora sees a girl with long dark hair in a red-and-white striped sweater walking alone. She pulls on her cigarette, blows out the smoke, and watches the child shuffle down the sidewalk, books clutched to her chest.

"I see this little girl and I hope people don't use her and abuse her,'' she says. ''I wonder what she's going to be like."

Susan Scora wants to open the window and shout to the girl with the message of her life: Be careful. It can happen to you.

May 24, 1993

Faces and Places: Maurice's Market

On a day still slapping at the snooze alarm, the RaceTrac gas station glows like a city on fire -- 20 gas pumps ablaze beneath a canopy of bright lights. Across some old asphalt, the Thrifty Mart with its three old-style gas pumps sleeps in the predawn darkness of Edgewater Drive. The storefront is decorated with signs of its three primary commodities: beer, cigarettes and lottery tickets.

At 5:55 a.m., Maurice Noujaim arrives to open the front door, just as he has for the past 34 years. He's a stout man with a bowling-ball belly, short legs with support socks pulled up to the knees, green Nike shorts and a white polo shirt with Citgo stenciled over the heart. A little American flag is pinned to his shirt pocket.

At 59, he works seven days a week because he lost his partner six years ago -- and because that's what it takes to survive in this business. In a city that grows larger every day, Maurice Noujaim's business is as small-town as they come. It's a little, overstuffed convenience store that acts more like an old-fashioned general store. He sells pork rinds, phone cards, scratch-off tickets and Mad Dog 20/20, but the store's true commodity is a sense of community.

"He's sort of the old grocer with a pencil behind his ear who knows everybody and takes care of them when times are bad. You don't find that anymore," said Frank Fondo, 51, a customer for 26 years.

RaceTrac is where you go for buck-fifty gas, a gallon of milk on the go and a bag of Krispy Kreme doughnuts. The place they call "Maurice's" is where you go for a familiar face, a sense of permanence, customer camaraderie -- or just to see Maurice.

And Maurice is always there, day and night. His image is imprinted on the minds of his regulars: bifocals on a tether like a school librarian; salt-and-pepper goatee, heavy on the salt; a voice that comes from a gravel pit some place in Lebanon -- rough in texture, but cordial in tone with an accent both foreign and familiar.

Most everybody who walks in the door, he calls by name.

"Good morning, how are you Charlie? . . . Good morning, Carol. How are you today? We have some fresh coffee . . . Herman, you doin' all right? . . . Bob, get a coffee . . . Good morning, Danny . . . Robert, you're looking good."

Maurice not only knows their names, but where they work, where they're going on vacation, if they had a birthday or a fight with their spouse, if they lost a job, if there's an illness in the family. He's a little bit bartender, little bit godfather, little bit banker. He cashes paychecks for the day laborers who work across the street.

For his regular customers who come up a little short, he keeps a tab -- scribbling their debt on a scrap of cigarette-carton cardboard. His business might be the last one on Earth that still offers full-service gas -- at no extra charge.

"We get a lot of old ladies. They come here for years and years. They don't know how to pump their gas. They don't know how to check their oil," he said.

His favorite customers -- black, white, Asian, Hispanic, gay or straight -- he calls "cuz."

"Everybody is Maurice's cousin. He doesn't discriminate against anybody," said Sue Hannah, 59, who owns the Faces lesbian bar across the street.

His is a working-class clientele, customers who come in with car grease on their hands, paint on their shirts, first names sewn on their shirts. For some, Maurice's is as much food pantry as convenience store. If he knows you, and you're hungry and broke, he'll provide food pro bono. Just ask.

But if you're hungry and broke and you try to shoplift, forget about it.

When the RaceTrac opened a few years ago, there were concerns it would siphon off his business. It's a familiar story -- big chain moves in, mom-and-pop store closes down.

But the old-fashioned way that Maurice conducts business produced another rarity these days: customer loyalty. To his regulars, patronizing RaceTrac is tantamount to betrayal.

"I'm sure RaceTrac is loaded with people new to town who go there because the gas is cheaper," Fondo said. "People who know Maurice would never do that."

For longtime customers, Maurice's is a landmark; Maurice, an institution. They can't imagine one without the other.

Maurice can. He's had four operations on his legs from standing behind that counter, 12 to 16 hours a day. He has a couple of daughters he still has to put through college, but after that, maybe it's time to try something else. For the past few years, he has been buying commercial property.

"I always do two things. If this one goes down the hole, I have something else," he said.

But Maurice in another line of business, or someone else owning Thrifty Mart, seems incomprehensible to his clientele. To them, the person and the place are the same thing.

"If Maurice was not there, it wouldn't be Maurice's any more. It would be like closing some historic site to me," said Bruce Sorensen, 45, a customer for more than 25 years.

At 10 p.m., there are still a couple of customers loitering inside the store when Maurice Noujaim turns off the beer signs in the front window, sets the burglar alarm and locks the front door. They part like old friends.

"See you tomorrow, Maurice."

"Good night, my friend.

It's dark inside the Thrifty Mart where the coolers hum a lullaby to themselves. Next door, at the discount gas station that never sleeps, the lights stay on all night.

April 28, 2003

Knock on Any Door: Six

If you are 6, and your name is James Cameron Martinez, anything you can catch is a potential pet. This is why you have a pet snail.

If you are 6 and starting first grade in a new school, you hold your own against the bad kid who tries to cut in front of you when you are lined up in Miss Miller's class.

"I was third in line, and he thought he was the third one. He thought he was the boss of me," Cameron says.

If you are 6, every loose tooth in your mouth is money in the bank. The front tooth you pulled out in class didn't hurt much or bleed. Once the Tooth Fairy retrieves it, you figure that tooth is worth four bucks. Your mom, Kami, kept the tooth in a plastic baggie in her jeans, until you insisted you wanted it and you put the tooth into the front pocket of your shorts. She told you to be careful not to lose it. But you did.

It was a very small tooth.

Any money you make from your missing teeth joins the thousands and thousands of pennies you have inside two small coin banks. If you had all the money in the world, you would spend it on Yu-Gi-Oh trading cards. You like playing with Yu-Gi-Oh cards and video games such as Ratchet & Clank, King Kong, and Halo. But the funnest thing of all is digging in the yard for fossils.

"Fossils are very hard to find," Cameron says. "You have to get really dirty."

Getting really dirty is one reason why it is better to be a boy than a girl. Boys can do whatever they want in their yards. Girls just play Gameboys all day. Boys catch lizards. Girls are afraid of lizards.

Your mother is afraid of alligators. You are not. If you saw an alligator, you would sock it in the eye with a board.

The only thing that scares you is haunted houses.

If you are 6, and your name is James Cameron Martinez, it is important that your friend next door, Amontae, is younger than you. Amontae is the best football player you know. Amontae is the best baseball player you know. Amontae is the best basketball player you know.

But Amontae is 5, and you are 6.

"He doesn't know how old I am," says Amontae. "I'm 6."

"No, you're not. You're 5," Cameron says.

"No, 6," Amontae says.

"Your mother knows how old you are," Cameron says.

"Yeah, 6," counters Amontae.

Closer interrogation discerns that Amontae's birthday is in September. He is almost 6.

"September is a long time. It's after August," Cameron says.

If you are 6, numbers are an abstract. The biggest number in the world is 103,000. You think your mother is 13. She says she is 26.

If you are 6, and your name is James Cameron Martinez, you have two fathers -- your biological dad and your stepdad. Neither lives with you. Your mother and stepfather divorced a year ago.

You moved into the three-bedroom, one-bathroom duplex apartment about a month ago. Your mother rides the bus to her job as a waitress. She doesn't own a car or a phone.

She walks you to school in the morning and picks you up in the afternoon. You make your own bed and choose your own clothes from two baskets on the floor -- one for shirts and one for shorts. After school, you get to pick a snack from Pop-Tarts, granola bars, fruit, yogurt and popcorn.

Your favorite food is sugar, because your mom says you can't have any. At night, your mother reads kids' versions of the classics to you. When she reads Treasure Island, she talks like a pirate.

Your mother thinks you are smart beyond your years. She says you tell funny jokes and make up elaborate stories about dinosaurs and monsters. She says you like to build things with Magneatos.

She thinks you will be tall and skinny. She thinks you might grow up to be an author or a builder. But her only ambition for you is that you are happy as an adult.

And she knows, as a woman who experienced heartbreak, that the one thing she wants most for you is the one thing she can't give you. Nobody can make you happy, she says. Things can't make you happy. You have to find it inside yourself.

You'd just be happy to find a fossil inside the backyard.

If you are 6, and your name is James Cameron Martinez, the animal you would most want to be is a shark. Because they tear things up.

And if you were a plant, you would want to be a flower. Because your mother loves flowers.

August 27, 2006

Knock on Any Door: Flower Lady

Mary Louise Patterson, who suffers from back pains and arthritis, sits on a chair to trim bushes in her yard. When she gives away her flowers, she said it helps her heal.

"Being nice to people helps a lot with my pain," she said. "When my mind feels good, my body feels good."

Some people in her neighborhood say they have never received roses from anyone but Patterson.

Mary Louise Patterson says tending to her flowers helps her forget her many health problems. In her purse, Mary Louise Patterson carries a credit-card-size X-ray of her spine like some parents carry ultrasound pictures of their unborn babies.

What the laminated X-ray shows is the lower vertebrae of her back encased in a cage of metal rods and screws. What it doesn't show is the degenerating discs and pinched nerves in her back, the arthritis in her shoulders and joints, the disintegrated cartilage in her right knee, and the four surgeries on her feet.

It doesn't show the betrayal of her body and the pain that it inflicts on a woman neighbors call The Flower Lady.

Mary Patterson's health problems come from more than 30 years of standing on her feet as a hairstylist, a beautician for funeral-home corpses, and a snack-food inspector at Frito-Lay. Where once she could stand for 12 hours a day, today she can only be on her feet for a few minutes at a time.

"I can't stand long. I can't sit long. And I can't lie in one place long," said Patterson, 63. "I have to move around. I get in my yard."

Her yard is not the marvel of manicured grass, neatly trimmed bushes and lush bunches of flowers it was when people used to approach Patterson and ask if they could get married in her back yard. After back surgery in 2001, Patterson has had to simplify her landscaping -- replacing annuals with perennials, substituting square blocks for grass.

Yet Mary Patterson's front yard remains a landmark in Richmond Heights, where even schoolchildren are awed by its beauty. When in full bloom, the yard is a painter's palette of red, blue, orange, yellow, pink, lavender and white.

"My health is failing me, but I still have a beautiful yard," she said. "I've never had an ugly yard."

There are things flowers can do for her that doctors can't. A rose, it turns out, is a powerful thing, more potent than a pharmaceutical company when it comes to controlling the pain that lives inside the bones and muscles of Mary Louise Patterson.

It's while she is working in her yard that the maladies of her body seem to fade away. For a little while, as she pulls weeds or prunes roses, her feet don't hurt, her back doesn't complain.

"It takes my mind off my problems because I'm concentrating on what I'm doing in my yard," she said. "It's therapy for the mind and the body."

While she works in her yard, Patterson is as attuned to her body as she is to leaves and petals, roots and branches. At the first tingle of fatigue, she puts down the garden trowel, strips off the rubber gloves and retreats inside the white and blue-trim house where she has lived for 38 years to rest and recover.

She has a son who could help her with the gardening, but he doesn't have her interest in the beauty of plants or her fine touch with vegetation. She loves him, it's true, but there are limits to even a mother's love.

"I don't want him messing up my flowers," she said.

There is respect on the street for Patterson's love of beauty. Her house has been burglarized, but even the punks leave her yard alone. Everybody in the neighborhood knows that when Patterson's yard blooms everyone benefits. Flowers aren't for the selfish. The beauty that relieves Patterson's pain also bestows pleasure when shared with others up and down the block.

"When my roses are blooming real good, a lot of the neighbors get bouquets from me, uh-huh," she said. "If I want to lift somebody's spirits, I cut them a bouquet. I think every neighbor around me has received a bouquet. Some more than once."

Mamie Forbes, 59, has received more flowers from Patterson than she has from her husband.

"I don't give her flowers," said Lewis Forbes, 66. "I give her hedges."

Another neighbor, Laureen Smith, gets candy from her husband of 57 years, but roses and Easter lilies from Mary.

"I like flowers. I love flowers. But I can't grow them myself," said Smith, 71. "I don't have the green thumb she has."

Some people in the neighborhood have never received roses from anyone but Mary Patterson.

"You can see the feeling in that person. They don't even need to say anything. The eyes glow," she said.

She tends to her flowers like she is raising a family. They are precious to her, but never so valuable that they can't be given away.

"I grow these flowers, but they're never too special that I can't pluck one and give it to somebody to make them feel better," she said. "You don't wait for somebody to die to give them flowers."

When The Flower Lady gives away her flowers, she also gives away a little of her own agony. There is an act of healing that comes with the gift of giving.

"Being nice to people helps a lot with my pain," she said. "When my mind feels good, my body feels good."

For many in Richmond Heights, life is hard and full of pain. But because of one woman's belief in beauty, the world seems a little less mean and smells a little sweeter.

September 5, 2004

Red Rountree: Bank Robber

Red Rountree left the old brown Ford pickup idling, the tank full of gas, in the NationsBank parking lot just a few blocks from the entrance ramp to Interstate 110.

It was a Monday, a little before 11 a.m., on Oct. 18, 1999. The day was warm and sunny as the tall, thin man with a white beard and long gray hair walked from his truck to the front entrance of the Pensacola bank.

Dressed in tan slacks and a gray shirt with red and white stripes, he carried a black leather tote bag in one hand and a handwritten note in his pants pocket.

Born in Texas, he was the last in his family, the sole survivor. Fay, his wife of 50 years, died of cancer in the 1980s. His stepson died in a car accident shortly after graduating from college. All four of his brothers were dead.

All gone, long gone, just like his life of affluence as a Houston businessman who designed and built industrial-sized cable winches that held offshore drilling rigs in place.

Walking into the bank, Rountree looked for the youngest teller and waited in line. When it was his turn, he gave her the note that said "Robbery" written in red ink.

"Give me the $100s," he told the bank clerk, and handed her the black bag.

Two months shy of his 88th birthday, Red Rountree was about to become one of the oldest bank robbers in American history.

"I rob banks for the money," Red Rountree says. "Social Security is all I have, and I like to live good."

The ID badge clipped to the collar of his blue prison shirt has his name misspelled. It says "Roundtree, JL Hunter." He tried to tell them, when he was being escorted into the North Florida Reception Center in Lake Butler, that there's no D in Rountree. He was told to shut up.

"In here," the corrections officers said, "your name is whatever we say it is."

As the oldest of 71,000 inmates in the Florida prison system, JL Hunter Rountree has learned to keep his mouth shut, do as he is told, and distance himself from other inmates and corrections officers.

"I get 10 days off a month for being a good boy. I'm going to continue being a good boy," says Rountree, sentenced to three years for the Pensacola bank robbery.

His hair, which he used to wear in a ponytail, is shorn prison-style short. His eyes are blue and small, sunken into his face like marbles dropped in mud. He wears large, prison-issued tortoise shell-framed glasses and a new pair of blue slip-on canvas shoes.

Rountree turned 89 on Dec. 16, 2000, a day that passed like all the others since he entered prison a year ago. No cake, no presents, nobody singing "Happy Birthday." No visitors.

"Prison is not so bad, but the food stinks," Rountree says.

He maintains his weight -- 166 pounds -- by drinking the nutritional supplement Ensure: "That's what keeps me going."

When he gets out of prison, Rountree says, he's going to buy a steak so tender you can cut it with a fork. He'll also have a salad, baked potato with all the goodies and a good glass of wine: "I've been accustomed to having food that is the best money can buy."

"Both JL and Fay had good taste and liked expensive things," said Betty Rountree. "They did all the things that people who had a lot of money did."

Betty's husband, Buddy Rountree, is Red Rountree's 71-year-old nephew, the only relative with whom he maintains a relationship. Buddy and his wife haven't seen Rountree since he stopped by their house in Goldthwaite, Texas, on his way to see a 30-something girlfriend serving time for drugs at the state prison in Gatesville.

"The last time we saw him in '95, he had a long ponytail and he was not the man that he once was," Betty Rountree said. "He was dressed more in what we would call hippie fashion than the very expensive attire that was his normal dress."

The man they knew was an educated, successful

businessman born in 1911 to a Texas sharecropper so poor he paid his debts by naming his son "JL" after the dry goods store owner and "Hunter" after the grocery store owner.

In the 1960s, Red Rountree made his fortune by building Rountree Machinery Co. from scratch to a thriving business with 75 employees. His homes in Houston were palatial.

"His house, to us, it was an elegant home," said Betty Rountree. "Everything was beautiful and expensive. They had someone keeping their yard."

Nicknamed for his red hair, Rountree married Fay, a petite, sophisticated woman, in 1936. It was a 50-year love affair. Her death from cancer in 1986 devastated him.

"After she died, I went crazy," Rountree says. "I was the most lonesome man you ever saw in your life."

He stopped associating with friends. Neglected his business. Started spending time in bars.

"When Fay died, he got to messing around with those younger women. I told him, `You are just messing with fire, JL,' " Buddy Rountree said. "Somebody his age could be influenced by a younger woman to do anything."

A year after Fay's death, Rountree married a woman he met at a bar. He was 76. She was 31. Later, he found she was addicted to cocaine and heroin.

"Before I met her, I thought drugs were something you get a prescription for," Rountree said. "She taught me different."

Rountree says he spent $500,000 putting his second wife through a series of drug rehabilitation programs -- depleting his fortune. After a couple of years, he divorced the second wife and began seeing another younger woman, the one in prison for drugs.

It was sometime in this period of his life -- he won't say when or where -- that Red Rountree robbed his first bank. Money was one reason. Revenge was the other.

"A Corpus Christi bank that I'd done business with had forced me into bankruptcy. I have never liked banks since," he said. "I decided I would get even. And I have. Banks are the easiest things in the world to rob."

On Dec. 9, 1998, while Rountree was holding up a bank

in Biloxi, Miss., a customer at a drive-through teller called the police on his cell phone. Arrested as he left the bank, Rountree was given three years probation, ordered to pay a $260 fine and told to leave the state of Mississippi. He was 87 years old.

Released from the Biloxi jail in August 1999, Rountree returned to Bayou La Batre, Ala., where he had been living in a travel trailer on property owned by Gilbert Diaz, a former customer. He bought the old Ford pickup for $3,500 from a friend of Diaz. Two months later, Rountree was in Pensacola looking for a bank close to the interstate.

"In all these years I have known him, I would not take him to be a person who would rob a bank. He dressed well, he had money, respectability," said Diaz, who first met Rountree in the 1970s. "I believe he lost his mind."

The nervous, shaken NationsBank teller stuffed $8,000 worth of $100 bills into Red Rountree's black leather tote bag, and he turned to walk nonchalantly out of the Pensacola bank.

Before he made it to the front door, a bank employee began to scream, "We've been robbed!"

Two customers in line behind Rountree began chasing him as he headed across the parking lot to the idling Ford pickup. Another man joined in the pursuit. He wasn't hard to catch.

"He was trying to run, but it was more like shuffling -- small, fast steps," said Samuel Goodwin, one of the customers who helped catch Rountree.

Knocked to the ground with a karate kick to the chest, Rountree was turned on his stomach and had his arms pinned behind his back by the customers. He was taken back inside the bank where he was held until the police arrived. While he was there, he crumpled up the robbery note and tossed it behind a desk, where police later found it.

"All of us were shocked to see someone that old involved in a crime like this," said Pensacola Police Lt. Bob Cotita. "I'd say he's a little old to be robbing banks."

Scheduled for release from Florida's prison in July 2002, JL Hunter Rountree will be returned to Mississippi for violation of his probation. It will be up to Circuit Judge Jerry O. Terry to decide if he would spend the next three years in a Mississippi prison.

"When I get out of here, they will give me a pair of clean pants, a blue shirt, a pair of shoes and $80. That's all I'll have," Rountree said. "I'll be 90 years old. What does a 90-year-old man do? Nothing."

Red Rountree is as unrepentant as he is candid about a life that has taken him from the cotton fields of Texas to the high life of Houston to the steel bars of a Florida prison where the food is lousy, but, he says, it's better than being in a nursing home.

He talks of getting a lawyer to sue the good Samaritans who tackled him in the parking lot: "They had no right to touch me." He talks of buying a van, fixing it up so he can live inside and just hitting the road. He talks of things he might do if he doesn't die in prison.

"I might rob another bank," he says. "I'm not saying I will or I won't. But, hey, I might need to."

February 4, 2001

Profile: Governor Farris Bryant

Black waiters circle the white linen tables, filling coffee cups and water glasses in the Jacksonville Omni ballroom packed with lunching Rotarians.

Farris Bryant sits at one of the tables among people he hardly knows. He is 86 years old with a feathery fringe of white hair and hearing aids in both ears. His jaw juts from his face and the corners of his mouth turn down naturally, making him look sad even when he isn't. In his younger days, people mistook him for Eisenhower.

But most of the people in the room are too young or too new to the Sunshine State to recognize Bryant as a former Florida governor.

He was a man of his time, and that time passed, leaving him a stranger in the state he helped to transform. He lives in the present, but the past still resides inside him, the long lost days of the segregated South when black and white lived by the unspoken codes of conduct and blatant signs that said White and Colored.

He has witnessed tremendous change sweep across Florida and the rest of the South, yet remains convinced that race relations in the United States haven't significantly changed since the 1960s.

A man alone in a crowded room, Bryant looks around for friends and old acquaintances. At another table he sees banker Chauncy Lever, who greeted Bryant outside the ballroom with a vigorous handshake.

"I liked the Florida when you were guvnah," Lever said. "You were a great guvnah."

Bryant was governor from 1961-1965, as tumultuous a time as any in Florida's history — short of that unfortunate conflict between the states 100 years earlier. The Cold War was in full bloom with the Cuban missile crisis unfolding 90 miles off Florida's coast. The civil rights movement was heating up with Freedom Riders flowing in from Northern states and Martin Luther King Jr. marching in St. Augustine. The space race against Russia was escalating with the construction of Kennedy Space Center in

Brevard County. Waves of new residents moving into Florida at the rate of 700 a day were creating the demand for more highways, more universities, more state parks.

Bryant governed when white men ruled, especially in the South. And it's that world where he remains most comfortable. He prefers those places — the weekly Rotary meetings and the dark-wood dining room of the Jacksonville Yacht Club — where people still greet him, "Hello, governor." He wears the title like a medal pinned to his chest.

"You never get over being governor," he said.

Thirty-five years removed from his term as Florida's 34th governor, Farris Bryant lives alone in a long riverfront condominium created by connecting two adjoining units in the Ortega Yacht Club Condominiums. He tends to his million-dollar portfolio from a room that is as much a museum as a study — walled in by photographs of him with Harry Truman, John F. Kennedy, Lyndon B. Johnson and Richard Nixon; multiple binders of photographs, letters and newspaper clippings; hardbound biographies, books on politics, race relations and communism.

Taped to the door of his den is a cartoon that says, "Well, here I sit, surrounded by my memorabilia, and I can't remember having done a damn thing."

What Bryant did, in no small part, was lay the groundwork for the Florida of today. His impact ranges from the pine-studded campus of the University of Central Florida to the long wide scar across the middle of the state that was once the Cross Florida Barge Canal to the sunken Christ of the Deep statue at the John Pennekamp Coral Reef State Park in the Keys to the over-used, often-cursed Interstate 4.

But Bryant remains best known as the segregationist governor who followed popular, progressive LeRoy Collins, much as Lester Maddox is remembered as Jimmy Carter's predecessor in Georgia.

Bryant, like other Southern governors at the time, believed that black and white children should be separated in school, that restaurant and motel owners had the right to pick their customers, and that racial equality would be achieved by changing people — not laws.

"Bryant will always be tar-brushed by his stance on civil rights," said Gary Mormino, a history professor at the University of South Florida. "He may be remembered more kindly in the future for creating a modern infrastructure for Florida, but the racial issues still haunt Bryant."

More than two-thirds of the state's 15 million residents were not living in Florida when Bryant served. With each passing year, as the state grows larger and more diverse, Bryant's circle of friends and admirers becomes smaller.

"I suspect not one in 1,000 Floridians remembers Farris Bryant, the state has changed so much," Mormino said.

At this stage, Bryant cares a great deal about whether he is remembered, and how.

"All I have left," he said, "is my reputation."

He has donated hundreds of thousands of dollars to the University of Florida for the preservation of his papers and political artifacts — to ensure that his legacy of achievement will not fade to yellow and turn to dust.

Bryant fears his reputation as a segregationist will stain that legacy like spilled wine on a white tablecloth — yet he remains true to beliefs he has held for a lifetime. He is a man both complicated and conflicted, entering the final years of his life without the guidance and companionship of the one true pure love in his life — his wife.

"She and I were one person," Bryant said. "To lose her was hell."

Julia Bryant's death from cancer at 78 in 1996 left Bryant grief-stricken, lonely, lost and disoriented. His depression was so deep it bore holes in his mind.

"Doctors say that if a person grieves like I did it will destroy some of the brain cells," Bryant said. "I experienced that, and I've been trying to build it back."

He still remembers this: the first time he saw her.

"She was the most gorgeous girl I had ever seen," Bryant said.

Julia Burnett was a young, brown-haired woman from a Panhandle family of politicians. Bryant was a 26-year-old newly minted Harvard law graduate with political ambitions inherited from his mother. They met at a Tallahassee tennis court where Julia invited Farris and a friend to join her and a date for a game of doubles.

Bryant took an immediate dislike to Julia's doubles partner.

"I was not very courteous. I was mean," Bryant said. "I tried to hit him with the tennis ball as hard as I could. It made him look bad."

After the match, Bryant asked Julia out. On their first date, he proposed. On the third, she accepted. They were married for 56 years.

Julia, a schoolteacher, tutored her husband on the fine points of politicking in public. A shy, uncharismatic person, Bryant made a poor candidate. When he would hesitate to approach voters, Julia would give him a gentle shove in the back. When he was giving a speech, sometimes standing on the back of a pickup truck, she would tug on his coat to remind him to address those standing behind him. Throughout their years together, Julia Bryant stood behind her husband, gently, persistently prodding Farris to step forward and speak up.

"She was wonderful for him. She was a better politician than he was," said former U.S. Senator George Smathers, who met Bryant when both were students at the University of Florida in the 1930s.

Julia took over the maternal mentoring role from Bryant's mother, Lela. Lela Bryant's influence on her son was immediate. Born on July 26, 1914 in Ocala's Marion General Hospital, Cecil Farris Bryant was named after his father, but was always known by his mother's maiden name — Farris.

In return, Farris Bryant always called his mother "Dearest."

Lela Bryant (a teacher just like Julia) had two ambitions for her son: to become well educated and be elected governor of Florida. She wanted him to succeed where her favorite brother, Ion Farris, failed when he ran for governor in 1910.

"My mother never wavered in her aspirations for me," Bryant said. "She had decided I was going to be governor, and I always assumed I would be. Dearest knew what should be."

Bryant's father, an accountant, had other plans for his son. Cecil Bryant wanted Farris to join him in his Ocala firm. In 1931, Farris Bryant enrolled at Atlanta's Emory University — which his mother considered the best school in the South — to study accounting: "Daddy wanted me to be an accountant, and I was going to be an accountant."

In the summer after his freshman year, Bryant fell in love with a girl in Ocala. On the train back to Atlanta, he got off at Gainesville, just north of his hometown. The romance went nowhere, but Bryant stayed in Gainesville and, unknown to his parents, enrolled in the University of Florida.

Since he chose to change schools without consulting his parents, Bryant felt they should no longer be responsible for his education. He worked his way through school, typing term papers, running a door-to-door fraternity dry cleaning service and a Greek Row candy-bar concession — demonstrating an early touch for making money.

Smathers recalls college-boy Bryant as bright, articulate, introverted and serious: "He was a smart guy, but he never indulged in jokes and tricks. He only talked business."

Bryant remembers himself as a less than brilliant student who worked hard to get good grades and, by some miracle, ended up attending Harvard law school. His roommate, a kid from Maine named Dan Gurney, would later become U.S. senator from Florida by defeating LeRoy Collins in 1968.

"My mother selected it, but I have always been puzzled how I got into Harvard. I don't remember applying," Bryant said.

Harvard, that bastion of liberal enlightenment, did not change Farris Bryant's conservative rural South politics. But it had an effect on Bryant that would separate him from other segregationist governors. Unlike Mississippi's Ross Barnett, Alabama's George Wallace and Georgia's Lester Maddox, Bryant was an educated, intellectual man who approached issues, including civil rights, from the head instead of the gut.

Bryant was neither a demigod like Wallace, an ax-handle waving cartoon character like Maddox, nor a venom-spewing racist like Barnett. Although a staunch segregationist, Bryant eventually joined the administration of Lyndon B. Johnson, a

Southern liberal, and enjoyed a good working relationship with John F. Kennedy.

"I don't see him in the mold of Lester Maddox. I don't see him raising the ire of the white masses against desegregation. Nor do I see him as a confrontational governor," said David Colburn, a historian at the University of Florida.

Following graduation, Bryant took a job with the Florida comptroller's office as an auditor. After he met and married Julia, they moved back to Ocala where Bryant opened a law office, joined the Elks, the Rotarians, and became Chamber of Commerce president.

In his first political race, with Julia quietly coaching in the background and his mother Dearest parked outside the newspaper office where the precinct totals were posted, Bryant won a seat in the Florida House of Representatives. The election was in November 1941. The next month, Japan bombed Pearl Harbor and the United States entered World War II.

Forsaking his seat, Farris Bryant resigned without setting foot in the House to join the Navy. Bryant's mother died while he was stationed in Guam — 15 years before he fulfilled her ambition for him to become governor.

"The Red Cross man walked up to me. I think I was on the beach. And he said, `I have some bad news for you.' I didn't know if it was my wife, or my baby, or my mother," Bryant recalled. "It was my mother. It was quite a shock."

After the war, Bryant returned to Ocala and won five terms to the Florida House, including a stint as speaker. He ran for governor in 1956 and lost, coming in third.

In 1960, the same year that JFK was elected president, Farris Bryant faced Doyle E. Carlton Jr., a moderate candidate handpicked by outgoing governor Collins, in the Democratic primary that would determine the state's next governor. In a debate, both men were asked whether they would pull their children from public schools if the courts ordered desegregation.

"I said no. I believed in strong public education and keeping the schools opened," said Carlton. "He said yes he would."

In a repudiation of Collins' moderate racial policies,

Florida voters overwhelmingly chose Farris Bryant.

"Bryant won," said historian Colburn, "because of increasing white resistance to the desegregation that was occurring throughout the South and Florida."

***

In the basement of the Governor's mansion is a 403-square-foot storage room filled with bottled water, paper towels, punch cups and old file folders containing dusty records. The room beneath Gov. Jeb Bush's front porch has been there since 1961 when fears of nuclear attack from the Soviet Union prompted the state of Florida to build a bomb shelter for Farris Bryant and his family. The room was divided in half — one side as living quarters for the Bryant family, the other half stocked with communications equipment and large enough to hold Cabinet meetings.

"The scary part was not the shelter itself, but the fact that it made the missile crisis real to a teenager," said Bryant's daughter, Cecilia, who was 15 years old at the time. "Watching supplies put into the shelter — beds, radio equipment — suddenly presented the possibility that the shelter might be used."

Less than a year after its completion, the governor's fallout shelter looked like a shrewd precaution. The Cuban missile crisis permeated America in the fall of 1962 when Kennedy went toe-to-toe with Nikita Khrushchev over the removal of Russian missiles on Cuban soil. The Cold War became suddenly superheated.

Nowhere did the threat seem so near, and so real, as Florida. It became Farris Bryant's role to work with Kennedy to prepare the state for war while urging Floridians not to panic.

"The thing I remember about the Cuban missile crisis was flying down to Key West in the president's plane, Air Force One, and getting out of the plane and walking along where all the planes were lined up across the field," Bryant said.

The United States was preparing to invade Cuba, if necessary, to destroy the Soviet missile bases. Bryant offered

Kennedy his advice — attack Cuba: "I said to the president, `You better do it now.' But I was wrong, and he didn't do it now."

After three tense months, the Cuban missile crisis ended when an U.S. naval blockade forced the Soviet Union to withdraw its missiles from the island, and Kennedy agreed to remove U.S. missiles from Turkey. The crisis passed, but the fallout shelter and the "Florida Center for Cold War Education" created by Bryant to spread anti-communism propaganda stayed.

With Florida no longer under threat of nuclear attack from Cuba, Bryant turned his attention to the deplorable state of Florida's highways and colleges. Florida, the nation's 10th largest state, ranked 49th in federal highway funds. Working with Kennedy and Smathers, Bryant leapfrogged Florida to No. 1 in highway funding with plans for extending Florida's Turnpike from Fort Pierce to Wildwood, construction of Interstate 4, Interstate 10, Alligator Alley and Interstate 75.

Then, combining his degrees in law and accounting, Bryant devised a way to fund the expansion of the state university system from four institutions to eight, including Florida Technological University that later became the University of Central Florida. He did so by convening a Council of 100 business leaders in the state who pushed for a constitutional amendment that raised bonds for the construction of colleges and universities. The amendment not only passed, but has since raised billions of dollars in construction funds for higher education.

"Building the higher education system and his efforts to diversify the state's economy were his two key successes for which he will be remembered," Colburn said.

Bryant promoted Florida tourism throughout the world, lured major league baseball to the Sunshine State for spring training, and courted industry to relocate in Florida. It was during Bryant's tenure that Walt Disney began scouting the state for his theme park. Bryant was also a big-time booster of the space program and the impact it would have on Central Florida by developing a highly trained and well-educated workforce.

"We will completely remake the face of Central Florida and affect the economy and society of the entire state," he proclaimed in the early '60s. "Florida is going to make the moon our 68th county."

Anticipating Florida's growth, Bryant also saw the need to save the state's natural resources. He established a revenue bond program for the purchase of endangered lands — among them the coral reef off Key Largo that became the John Pennekamp State Park.

But Bryant ran into opposition from environmentalists who opposed the creation of the Cross Florida Barge Canal, which the governor pushed as a shortcut for ships that would reduce truck traffic on the state's highways. Environmentalists claimed the canal was an ecological disaster that would sever Florida in half. Backed by Lyndon Johnson, the controversial project limped along for eight years until Richard Nixon halted it with an executive order in 1972.

By the time his four years were up, Farris Bryant had effectively altered the landscape of Florida for generations to come.

"Florida was at a turning point," Bryant said. "It was just coming into its own."

Limited by the Florida constitution to one term as governor, Bryant joined LBJ's administration as director of emergency planning after leaving office. In 1970, he made a run for the U.S. Senate, but lost to Lawton Chiles.

Florida had changed. Farris Bryant had not.

***

Three and a half decades after Farris Bryant was governor, tens of thousands of blacks marched on Tallahassee to oppose Gov. Bush's "One Florida" plan to end affirmative action in college admissions. In South Carolina, crowds of civil rights activists protested the Confederate battle flag flying from the dome of the state capitol.

It's been 36 years since Congress passed the Civil Rights Act. All restaurants, motels and public schools are integrated. Blacks and whites drink from the same water fountains, swim in the same pools, sit at the same lunch counters.

"I was not in favor of changing the laws. I was not in favor of the Civil Rights Act of '64," Bryant said, sitting in a floral upholstered chair in his Jacksonville study. "And look how it has turned out."

The way it turned out, in Bryant's eyes, is that integration in America is a thin veneer of social interaction. He believes blacks and whites are no closer to equality than they were in the 1960s: "We haven't given the Negro the same rights as a white man. There is a wide gap between that idea and reality."

Asked if he thought we had made progress in race relations over the past 40 years, Bryant replied, "I don't think we have."

Seated across from him was his daughter, Cecilia Bryant, a Jacksonville attorney who has stepped into the maternal caregiver role left behind by her mother. Cecilia stops by every day to check on her father. She brings him supper packed in Tupperware. She is his adviser, his confidant, his protector, his spin-doctor.

"Really, Daddy?" Cecilia Bryant said.

"Why do you think we have?" Bryant retorted.

"Well, I have so many black friends," Cecilia said.

"You've never brought any home," her father replied, tersely.

The world does not seem to have changed much to Farris Bryant because he has not changed much. For him, civil rights was — and still is — a question of property rights, not human rights.

"Part of his problem is he looked at issues on an intellectual basis when they were not issues you could separate from the emotional," said John E. Evans, a former aide.

Freedom, Bryant contends, is the right of a property owner to use that property — be it a motel, restaurant, or home for sale — as he or she sees fit.

"I believe the Negro race would proceed in their pursuit of civil rights faster by changing the minds of the white people — not by forcing them to do something by taking their property away from them," Bryant said.

In 1961, Bryant testified before Congress, "When the

majority loses its freedom, the minority loses its hope of freedom."

To this day, Farris Bryant has a hard time understanding how his view of human relations — of commerce above dignity — failed.

"My argument, which is logical, is a bad argument," Bryant concedes. "And I don't see why it is."

Despite his opposition to the civil rights movement, Bryant believed that his duty as governor was to prevent Florida from erupting into flames and blood — to figuratively step between black civil rights activists and white racists to preserve order. When the Freedom Riders came to Florida, Bryant orchestrated a behind-the-scenes plan to avoid conflict as the buses rolled across the Panhandle. Bryant ordered Florida Highway Patrol troopers to persuade owners of restaurants and bus depots all along North Florida to either serve the activists or close down instead of refusing them service.

"When they drove into town and headed for the bus stop they would find nothing to fight about," Bryant said. "They could go into the bus station, order what they wanted, and be served by people willing to do it."

The tactic worked. There were no riots, arrests or bloodshed. The Freedom Riders passed from Jacksonville to Tallahassee and everywhere they stopped, they received service in restaurants and bus stations where blacks were traditionally excluded.

"I didn't let it come to a confrontation," Bryant said. "That was the difference between Florida and other states. I never did anything except try to avoid conflict."

Bryant's civil rights strategy was to give protesters their platform without making any concessions that would trigger a racist backlash. He refused to meet with Martin Luther King Jr., when the civil rights leader led marches in St. Augustine to integrate the city's motels. But Bryant sent his emissaries to coordinate events with King.

"We had undercover people out with the Klan so we knew what they were doing. And we had people working with King to see what he was doing," said Evans, who was sent to St.

Augustine by Bryant. "We didn't want riots, and we didn't want conflict."

Bryant was different from other Southern segregationist governors, in part, because Florida was different from other Southern states. In the 1960s, Florida was the only Southern state that was gaining population. And most of that growth was from Northerners — many of them moving to Florida to retire.

Nor did any other state rely on tourism to the extent Florida did. Image was important to Florida's economy and Farris Bryant understood that.

"In many ways, he was trapped by history," said history professor Mormino. "He was deeply conflicted, struggling between the Florida that was very Jim Crow Southern and the new Florida that was emerging — tourism, high technology, Cape Canaveral."

With his heart in the old South and his head in the new Florida, Bryant chose a middle ground between those who vehemently opposed integration and those who advocated change. Bryant did nothing to advance school desegregation in Florida, but he also didn't stand in the schoolhouse door, as Wallace did, or personally chase away blacks trying to integrate restaurants as Maddox did.

But to blacks in Florida, Bryant's election was a step back from the civil rights policies of LeRoy Collins.

"I didn't think much of any Southern governors at that time. Bryant was just another racist governor," said James Eaton, history professor at Florida A&M University and a civil rights activist in the '60s. "Racism was so widespread there was nobody who was white I could single out who would take a stand for African-Americans in Florida."

Where Eaton agrees with Bryant, however, is that the civil rights movement did not produce equality between blacks and whites. Moreover, there's evidence of America moving away from the gains made during the '60s, said Eaton, who views Gov. Jeb Bush's "One Florida" plan to end affirmative action in college admissions as an attempt to return to the past.

"I think Farris Bryant is right. We are still struggling. We are still marching," Eaton said. "Conservative is a catchword for turning the clock back."

Bryant himself, unapologetic about his past as a segregationist, feels he should be remembered as the governor who kept Florida from being ripped apart by racial conflicts while the rest of the South was busting heads, bombing churches and shedding blood.

"My purpose where civil rights were concerned was designed to preserve the peace. As governor, that was my job. And I did that," he said. "Florida did not become a battleground."

***

In April 1995, Farris and Julia Bryant were preparing for another cruise. The Bryants loved to sail on the all-inclusive cruise lines where customers are pampered without having to ever remove their wallets.

Since leaving the governor's mansion, Bryant had amassed a fortune with a Jacksonville corporate law practice and an insurance company he formed. He owned yachts and a summer home in the North Carolina mountains, a house on a lake near Ocala and the sprawling condo overlooking the Ortega River in Jacksonville

Bryant accumulated his wealth with the idea that his estate would provide a comfortable living for Julia and their three daughters, Julie, Cecilia and Adair, after his death.

"I always planned to die early. My family all died early," Bryant said. "My wife, she came from a long-lived family. And that's what she expected."

Neither was prepared when doctors diagnosed Julia Bryant with cancer in 1995.

"The thought of her dying was just repulsive to me. I couldn't bring my mind around it," Bryant said.

From the moment of Julia's diagnosis to the time of her death, Farris Bryant was his wife's caregiver. He fed her, bathed her, dressed her. Hospice workers came, but she sent them away, wanting and needing only her husband at her side. Bryant reveled in his role, the opportunity to administer to his wife as she had always looked after him.

"I told her, `I love taking care of you.' And I did," Bryant said. "My only thing was to make the last months of her life pleasant. I would not let her suffer."

When it became clear that the cancer was incurable, Bryant wanted to take his wife on one last ocean cruise. The doctors said no. When he knew she didn't have much time left, he wanted to rent a RV with a bed and drive them to their home in Cashiers, N.C., where they could sit one last time on the chairs that overlook the mountains. The doctors said no. He obeyed the doctors and regrets that he did.

"I hate those doctors," he said.

Julia Bryant died on Sept. 8, 1996 with her family gathered around her hospital bed. She is buried in a cemetery in her hometown of Madison. Once a month, Farris Bryant drives the 200-mile round trip to visit her grave.

"I talk to her. I don't think she's there, but that's as close as I can get," he said.

At night, Bryant works his way through a 20-volume interpretation of the Bible and thinks he can sometimes feel her presence in the words.

There's a large oil painting of Julia Bryant on the dining room wall of their condo. She has brilliant blue eyes, auburn hair, a dark, V-neck dress and pearl necklace. One hand hangs over the arm of the chair, the other lies casually in her lap. The portrait was painted in 1961, Bryant's first year as governor.

"Isn't she beautiful?" Bryant said. "She was feeling bad that day. She didn't want to have her picture made."

The look on her face is one of serenity and confidence.

When she died, in a way, so did he.

"Julia had a year and a half after she was told she had cancer and it was hopeless. Instantly, the only thing you have to look forward to is today," Bryant said. "And when the spark is gone out of today, that's about it. There's no fun in life."

***

Farris Bryant Walks in anonymity past the park in the town square where the courthouse once stood. Fifty years ago, when he first opened his law practice in Ocala, Bryant would stroll around the square with his briefcase, up the steps of the courthouse, through the building and out the other side, just to be noticed.

The courthouse is gone now, torn down, another absence that makes Bryant feel like a stranger in his own hometown. A bank has replaced his father's accounting office. The old drugstore where he and his law partner would stop in for a five-cent Coca-Cola is a swanky Cajun-style restaurant with exposed brick walls and high ceilings.

Bryant wears a blue, button-down dress shirt, tan slacks, a necktie selected by Cecilia, and a gold tie tack with the initials CFB. On his left hand he wears his Harvard ring, class of '38.

He walks past a woman sitting on a park bench, fanning herself against the summer heat. He looks at her, she doesn't see him. He notes their lack of interaction as another sign that nothing is what it used to be.

"I would have known her and she would have known me," he says. "She would have spoken to me and I would have spoken to her and asked her if I could help."

But Ocala has become too big for that now. When Bryant was a boy, it was a town of 8,000. It's now a city of 50,000. He still has a few old friends in town, but not many.

"The ones who are here feel just as lost here as I do," he says.

Farris Bryant is a man who has lived long enough to be forgotten. The state he molded in his vision of the future has grown too big, too impersonal, too indifferent to its own past, to remember the man who believed he was born to be its governor.

As he drives around Ocala looking for landmarks of his past — his yellow-brick grade school and the First United Methodist Church he and his father helped build — Bryant turns down a narrow street of older homes designated by historic district signs. He drives slowly, looking for a small frame house where he once lived.

There's a young woman sitting on the front steps of a gray house reading a book. Farris Bryant stops the car and rolls down his window.

"Hi," he says.

The woman looks up, and then leaps to her feet.

"Granddaddy!" she says, coming toward him with open arms.

September 3, 2000

PLACES

On Any Given Sunday: Running of the Chihuahuas

Sandwiched between the Kentucky Derby on Saturday and Cinco de Mayo today, there was the Running of the Chihuahuas on Sunday.

This is what it looked like: 101 Chihuahuas, in heats of five, running, meandering and sniffing one another on a 30-foot raceway outside the Cocina 214 Mexican restaurant in Winter Park.

A couple of the dogs got to the checkered finish line and stopped short, uncertain whether it was safe to step on the black-and-white pattern. A few broke from the starting line and ran into the crowd. More than one made it halfway down the lane, thought better of it, and ran back the other way.

Six-month-old Lewie, who won his heat, lost in the semi-finals when he headed toward Cocina instead of the finish line.

"He went to the bar. It was Corona hour," said Gail Muringer, who owns Lewie and The Dog MaHall luxury pet hotel in Orlando.

The Chihuahuas were dressed in sequined collars, studded halters, colorful bandanas, frilly dresses and hand-made racing jerseys with their names on the back. Some wore small plastic sombreros, but not for long. They went by the names of Chi-Chi, Wa-Wa, Nacho, Charlie, Sammy, Saffron, Pepe and Señor Taco.

They were short-haired, long-haired, black, white, tan, brown, spotted, and ranged in size from 2 pounds to 15 pounds. Their owners were black, white, Hispanic, young, old, single, married, entire families, and enjoyed the festivities while sipping on drinks that ranged from frozen Margaritas to Mexican beer.

"What I love about it is you have so much diversity," said Cocina co-owner Labine Macejewski. "And the dogs, too."

The event raised $1,200 for Winter Park Lost Pets and A Cause 4 Paws Rescue.

The dogs -- at times antsy, distracted and disobedient -- were better behaved than some of their owners, who had to be repeatedly warned to stay behind the starting line and stop reaching for the dogs before they crossed the finish line.

The owners used various incentives to lure their pets to run:

squeaky toys, tasty treats and desperate pleas. One shook a baggie of dog biscuits, another held a chip made of chicken between her fingers.

While many were new to the Chihuahua racing racket, some dogs had competed last year, including Chiquita Banana, who failed to finish -- again.

"She got approximately 3 feet farther this year," said Elizabeth Fernandez, of Longwood.

Owners used different techniques for preparing their dogs to race.

"He chases squirrels in the park," said Kelsey Billings, of Orlando, owner of Bruiser.

"She's been training all year. We have a large backyard," said Melvin Gray, of Winter Park, owner of Peanut.

Gray and his wife, Karen, entered Peanut from their stable of three Chihuahuas.

"She's the fastest of the three," said Gray, of Winter Park.

But not fast enough.

In the end, a dog named Hemingway came out the winner, sprinting to the finish without detours or distractions. It was the first victory for Hemingway, a 2-year-old Chihuahua from Orlando.

In preparation for the race, Hemingway fetched balls in the backyard.

Hemingway also had been trained to come when Jessica Lapp -- mother of the dog's owner -- held her fingers to her mouth and whistled. In a race with a lot of spectators, shouts and smells, whistling seemed to provide the winning edge.

"When I call him, he knows I mean business," said Lapp. "There are consequences for being bad. No treats."

May 5, 2014

Faces & Places: Burton's Bar

In the light of a setting sun, the salons, restaurants and boutiques of Thornton Park glow bright through their plate-glass windows as if the stores themselves were streetlights.

The one exception on East Washington Street is Burtons Bar & Grill. The bar is dark, its windows illuminated by the neon of AmberBock and Budweiser signs. Even with the doors closed, you can smell the smoke and suds inside.

Back when John and JoAnn Wright bought the place in 1968, Burtons was a neighborhood bar. But the neighborhood has changed. The houses in Thornton Park sell for upwards of $300,000. Their owners prefer the upscale to the low-rent.

"It's never going to be a busy regular place for this neighborhood. It looks dark and scary to them. The young yuppies like lit-up places," says bartender Donna Milar, 56.

The walls have 1970s paneling. The jukebox plays the Righteous Brothers. Every booth has a black plastic ashtray. The menu is beef and grease. Cash only. You want to buy a beer with a credit card, go to the 7-Eleven down the street.

During the day, the bar is mostly empty except for old-timers such as Ray Beck, 68, and Carl Sandlin, 69, who gave up drinking but still come to Burtons for lunch. And Al Beaudoin, 46, who comes here when he doesn't want to be found.

The regulars have to go out of their way to get here. They come because it's a place they can't find in their own neighborhoods. They come because Burtons offers familiarity and cheap beer in a city that is often impersonal and increasingly expensive.

At one end of the bar is Dave Alexander, a 45-year-old cabdriver and occupational-therapy student who stops at Burtons on his way home to Avalon Park. There's a bar in Avalon Park, but it's too open, too bright, too noisy for Alexander.

Next to him is John Clarke, 38, who comes in with his dark blue T-shirt splattered with plaster from a day spent installing drywall. Burtons reminds Clarke of the Brookside bar back home in New Jersey that served as his hometown's community center. Parents brought their kids along when they went to the Brookside.

Then there's Easton Martin, 38, who drinks Bud by the pitcher. Martin is into the retro thing, and Burtons is as "old school" as they come.

At the other end of the bar is Roger Brown, 75, a former trucker with Karl Malden's nose and a small pitcher of AmberBock all to himself. Brown has been coming to Burtons since the 1970s, and it hasn't changed much since then. The Hotpoint deep fat fryer was here when the Wrights bought the place. The booths and bar stools were new 15 years ago. Some of the pool cues look like they've been chewed by dogs.

"Sometimes Budweiser puts a new sign in here. That's cause for celebration," Brown says.

It might just be a bar, like any other bar, but something more than beer and money is exchanged at Burtons. There is an intimacy between patron and owner that is rare these days.

JoAnn Wright is 72 but still opens Burtons every morning at 10 a.m. and works till 4 p.m., when Milar takes over. The regulars know all about Wright's family, and she knows all about them. She attends their weddings and funerals. She has given some jobs, given others money.

And they do things for her in return. Dave Linnan picks up her hamburger meat one day, brings in the buns the next day. They've gone to baseball games at Tropicana Field in St. Petersburg together.

One customer rebuilt the wood awning over the front of the bar and etched in it her husband's name at the peak of the façade and the year of his death: 1987. Another customer repaired the bar's plumbing, and another left JoAnn his collection of hand-made beer trucks.

But much of her regular clientele is dying off -- an occupational hazard for a business based on smoking, drinking and high cholesterol. People are more health-conscious these days. Dark, smoky bars are not the next big trend.

So along with the bar talk about the nature of inertia and whether Sammy Sosa used steroids, there is speculation as to how long Burtons will be around. Wright is coy about what will happen to the neighborhood bar. Rumors about Burtons flow like beer from the tap.

There are those who say Wright keeps the bar as a sentimental memorial to her husband. And others who say she promised him before he died from cancer that she would never sell the bar. Some think she just hasn't received the right offer yet, and others think that when the bar becomes a headache, she'll sell it. And still others insist that as long as there is a JoAnn, there will be a Burtons -- till death do they part.

A lot of wishful thinking goes on at Burtons, because it's the kind of business where the customers think the place belongs to them. And when it's gone, a piece of them will disappear as well.

January 8, 2005

Knock On Any Door: Poor

Here is what it is like to be poor.

You don't have money to replace the teeth missing from your mouth. You don't have the medical insurance to pay for the double hernia operation you need. Your son, who fell to his death 10 years ago, is buried in an unmarked grave because you never had the money for a tombstone.

You work hard for a company that makes spiral staircases for million-dollar homes. You come home to a single-wide, '70s-era trailer you rent for $120 a week. Your arms are streaked with dirt, dust, sweat and paint. The black beneath your fingernails is eternal.

You sit at the round plastic patio table in front of the trailer, open a Busch beer and drink from the can. You light a generic-brand cigarette with a green plastic Bic lighter.

You look around at the trailers full of people just like yourself. Roofers. Cabinet makers. Painters. Tree trimmers. Security guards. Lumberyard workers. The couple on disability. The two single fathers in a single-wide who work opposite shifts so they can watch each other's kids. The 24-year-old woman who works at a fruit-packing plant and temp jobs to support her kids, her sister and her mom.

You think about your own mother, who raised seven kids by herself. You shared a room with two other brothers. Your four sisters squeezed into another bedroom. Your dad . . . well, you never knew him.

You grew up poor in Muncie, Ind., but your mom, she always had a beautiful yard. You're poor in Orange County, but you also have a beautiful yard.

In all of the Lockhart Mobile Home Park, yours is the only trailer with a yard, a white wood fence and lawn statuary. The yard reflects your philosophy in life -- if you are poor and your name is Richard Brazzel.

"I know I am a poor man, but I do not have to live like one," Brazzel says. "You can have zero money in your pocket, but you don't have to look like it."

Brazzel, 56, brings home $15,600 a year from his job at an ornamental ironworks company. Some of that money goes toward making a rented trailer feel like a real home.

It took him a long time to break up and haul away the asphalt and gravel in front of his trailer. The sod he laid died. He planted grass seed; he fertilized. He sweated; he watered. The grass turned green. He surrounded it with the fence after he got tired of people driving over his lawn. He bought the statuary from F&F Concrete Products, which also owns the trailer park.

Two concrete Rottweilers guard the sidewalk leading to the front door of Trailer 17, where Brazzel, his wife, Trish, and their 17-year-old son, Christopher, have lived for the past eight years. There's a statue of an eagle, because Brazzel loves eagles. And a statue of two little kids kissing. And another statue of a little boy holding an umbrella over the head of a little girl who is crying.

"The little boy is saying, `Honey, don't worry. It's going to rain. Don't matter. Everything is going to be all right,' " Brazzel says.

Every life has its rainy days, its sorrows. Brazzel carries inside him the loss of his oldest son, a 22-year-old roofer and amateur rock-band drummer who liked to climb the silo of a concrete block company to look out at the lights of Orlando.

"He just liked to get up there and look over the world. It was his time to think. I guess everybody has to have a place like that," Brazzel says.

Ronald Lee Brazzel fell to his death on Aug. 7, 1995.

For a time after his son's death, Brazzel would sneak into the factory at night and arrange the concrete blocks into the shape of a cross. He doesn't do that anymore. He visits his son's unmarked grave and, instead of leaving flowers where the tombstone should be, he buries tapes and CDs of his son's favorite music -- Kid Rock, Black Sabbath, AC/DC. One cold winter, he covered the grave with a blanket.

He has buried the memory of his son's death deep inside him. It's in a place he doesn't visit too often. When he does, it starts him drifting. And when that happens, when the thoughts bring him too close to the pain, he brings himself back by thinking of what he still has, not what he lost.

He has his wife of 34 years, the woman he says holds his world together. Trish Brazzel is a good-hearted woman who has volunteered for 12 years at the Human Crisis Council, handing out free food.

He has three sons, one of whom has a dog that looks like the flesh-and-blood version of his concrete Rottweilers.

He has his yard. The yard is the place Brazzel goes when he wants to think -- or forget.

"Working around my yard keeps my mind off my everyday problems," he says.

Every March, on his birthday, Richard Brazzel takes a day off work. He spends that week's paycheck on ribs, chicken, pork chops, hot dogs and sausage. He lights up the big black metal grill. He feeds the trailer park.

And he counts himself a lucky man. Not a man with a lot of money, but a rich man nonetheless.

April 30, 2006

Kulture: Flat Tires, Fights, Falstaffs

OSTEEN – Kenny's Service Station was my kind of bar.

Beer was 65 cents. There were three pool tables and a few video games. The jukebox ran from hard rock to classic country. There was no cover charge. No ferns. If you wore a tie, you were suspected of being a narcotics agent.

In its day, Kenny's was the closest thing to a theme bar in this south Volusia County town of 4,000. Some folks spend big bucks to make their bars look like something they aren't -- English pubs, railroad stations, Western saloons. Not Kenny.

Kenny's bar was decorated in authentic Rural Automotive. Fan belts on the walls. Bare concrete. Exposed ceiling rafters. Sheet metal roof. The lounge furniture consisted of one black vinyl beanbag chair.

Kenny Patterson ran his business as a garage during the day and as a bar at night. From 8:30 a.m. until 6 p.m., he was an auto mechanic. From 6 to 10 p.m. on weekdays and until 2 a.m. on weekends, he was a bartender.

If you wanted to find Kenny's, you had to know where to look. There was no sign outside the building, nothing to distinguish it from any other three-pump country gas station except for the gaggle of cars parked outside after 6.

It was a bar that lacked pretensions. It was rough-hewn and rednecked. The bar's customers were mostly local and largely young, and that ultimately led to the bar's demise.

"For a time there, when I had the pool tables, it was making a lot of money," said Patterson, 33. "It was an unusual thing to have a bar in a garage. It attracted a crowd, a younger sort of rowdy crowd, an Osteen crowd.

"Then it started getting out of hand. They kept fighting. I told them to stop. After a while I had to put a lot of rules down, and some just couldn't abide by that."

By most standards, the rules were not oppressive. Kenny still didn't require his customers to wear shirts or shoes. But his patrons found the restrictions against foul language and barroom brawls too inhibiting.

Eventually they stopped coming back. Business

declined. The customers returned to the woods and parking lots to drink and fight. Kenny removed the video games and pool tables. The only evidence that the service station once played a dual role is a Miller Time sign next to the gaskets and a Natural Light beer clock above one window.

The bar has been shoved into the front of the building, where it is tended these days by Kenny's 62-year-old mother, Libby. A hand-lettered sign says "In God we trust. All others will pay cash." Beer is 80 cents. The regulars are mostly old-timers who talk about getting wound as tight as an eight-day clock.

Kenny has returned to fixing cars full time. The kids still come around to haggle over the price of a tire or get help in repairing a leaky valve stem. An occasional tourist, lured by the trailer sign that proclaims "Mechanic On Duty," pulls in to have a burned-out taillight bulb replaced.

Down the road, the Foxhead Lounge, which opened about the same time that Kenny's bar reverted to a service station a couple of years back, has a band on weekends, a pool table and a fist-hole in the restroom door. But the beers cost a buck and a quarter and you have to wear a shirt to get in.

November 17, 1985

It's Different Here: A Perfect Day

Monday was a day in the park, a walk around the lake, a picnic on a blanket, a table outside, please. It was hanging out the wash on Washington Street, cooking pork chops at Lorna Doone Park and being glad your flight back to Boston on Saturday was canceled.

It was a day in Central Florida that fell within the parameters of perfect: high in the 70s, low humidity, a flawless sky, a tickling breeze.

"It couldn't get any better than this," said attorney Jim Bacchus, 64, taking a work break to walk around Lake Davis in Orlando. "This is why God made Florida."

It was a day to rejoice, revel and gloat about being down here instead of back home in Chicago, Boston, New York, Atlanta or North Carolina.

"It's 19 degrees in Boston today," said Patricia Greener, 29, who is visiting her sister in Orlando. "The weather has been so bad, my flight was canceled. But that's OK with me."

Because it was Presidents Day, this perfect day fell on a Monday when kids were out of school and parents were home to take them on bike rides or toss a football.

"These are the days I cherish, my friend," said Gregg Saxonis, 51, a Maitland contractor who was lofting a football to his sons Devan, 7, and Kai, 6, while his wife was out running and their 9-year-old daughter Olivia was riding bikes with friends.

Dressed in a tank top, shorts, running shoes, and tattoos, Saxonis said his sister's kids in the Northeast are afraid they'll still be in school in July to make up for all the snow days this year.

"Look at this sky," he said. "It's like it's painted. It's beautiful. I don't ever want to go back to work."

Even chores -- all the lawn work put off by the recent weekends ruined by rain and cold -- were made better on a day like Monday. Steve Besedick, a 58-year-old dean at Winegard Elementary School in Orlando, was working in his brick courtyard, trying to fix a gas-powered edger on a day that included weeding the flower beds, cutting the grass and, hopefully, edging and trimming. His wife, Susan, was supervising.

"The past few weeks have been so dreary," said Susan Besedick, 53, a teacher at Winegard. "We have a lot of neglect out here."

The Besedicks are from Ohio, where the winter has been so bad the Great Lakes have frozen over for the first time in decades. It's easy to forget what it's like living up North -- the snow, the ice, the unrelenting cold -- and a little too easy to take a day like this one for granted, Susan said.

"When you have a day like this, we oftentimes are not grateful for it," she said. "It's like therapy for our stressful lives."

John Lee Turner, 70, enjoying a strawberry-flavored cigar on a bench in Parramore's Checker Park, feels the same way about his native Georgia, where snow and ice have shut down Atlanta twice this winter.

"It's snowing up North, but we're enjoying it down here," Turner said. "It don't get no better than this."

A perfect day like this is made all the more perfect knowing that in the next few days the temperature is expected to reach the 80s -- a reminder that winter in Central Florida is short-lived and summer is lurking.

"It's cold and hot, hot and cold," said Rodney Jones, 48, within smelling distance of the pork chops Terry Lovette was cooking for his family in Lorna Doone Park near the dismantling of the Florida Citrus Bowl. "This is the time of year when you catch the flu."

But this was not that day, a day of feeling sick and staying inside. This was a day for the outdoors, for walking the dog and pushing the baby stroller, for girls softball practice at Boone High School, and for getting the kids out of the house.

It was a day for Jennifer and Chris Douglass to play with their daughters, Adelle, 3, and Collette, 2, in the yard of their Orlando home -- Chris tossing Adelle into the air and swinging her around by the arms. It was a day for baking peanut cups and playing hopscotch and drinking mimosas outdoors.

To Jennifer, it felt like a Monday meant to be written down and preserved forever: "This day is like a poem."

February 18, 2014

Old Store

PEACHTREE, N.C. – Decades of dust shroud the glass counters containing hatpins, buttonhooks, and decorative hinges for homemade coffins. Left intact for more than 50 years, W.P. Brittain's one-room general store is a mercantile tomb of a time when folks paid for kerosene, lye soap and snuff with eggs, chickens and hickory nuts.

The store, opened in 1884, is stocked from floor to ceiling with the everyday essentials of life in rural western North Carolina: wooden barrels of horseshoes, flour and coffee; boxes of gun powder, buckshot and bullets; rows of glass canning jars; stacks of men's derbies, women's corsets and children's slate school tablets.

Everything is pretty much as Brittain left it after closing up shop one day in 1933 and falling ill. He never recovered, and the store never reopened. His daughter, Verdie Ledford, refused to sell the store or its inventory - preferring instead to keep it as her private warehouse and personal museum.

''She just wanted to leave it like her father had it,'' said Jerry Sudderth, who inherited the store in 1988. ''She revered the past. She didn't want to change anything.''

Sudderth shares his grandmother's reverence for the historic preservation of the family store. During the past two years he has unlocked the door to conduct tours back in time for about 700 people who have come from as far away as Utah. His price of admission is a genuine appreciation for old things.

''Everything in the country you have to pay to see,'' said Sudderth, 50, a machinist at a nearby electronics plant. ''But if someone is genuinely interested in seeing something old and appreciates something like this, we're happy to show it to them and not charge anything.''

There are no signs outside the store, nothing to indicate the two-story, white frame building is anything but a regular old barn nestled between a cemetery and a vegetable garden. But somehow people drawn to a lost way of life find their way to Sudderth's door in this small community near the north Georgia border.

Inside the store, they find a time capsule truer to life than any museum or nostalgic theme-park reproduction of turn-of-the-century America. There is nothing selective or sanitized about the old store. It's all authentic, right down to the dust on the countertops and the licenses on the wall for the sale of opium.

The narcotic drug was once an over-the-counter painkiller and primary ingredient in patent medicine. Labels on some of the medicine bottles state that the contents were 60 percent opium and 30 percent alcohol.

"No wonder they were such miracle cures," Sudderth said. "You could give someone a shot of that on their death bed, and they'd get up and fly away."

The currency of the day was barter. Coops in the back of the store were for the chickens and turkeys that people brought in to exchange for supplies like Dr. Caldwell's Laxatives, Bruton's Scotch Snuff for the Teeth, Gattis Worm Oil, Black Edge Gun Wads and Pflueger Fish Hooks (since 1864). On the floor are boxes of walnuts, hickory nuts and gourds, all traded in for merchandise from Brittain's store.

"A lady in her 80s told me that every fall her dad would bring a wagon load of corn to trade for shoes for the family," Sudderth said.

Even school children would come into Brittain's, looking to trade the hard-boiled eggs from their lunches for peppermint candy in the big glass jars.

The store has no electricity. A shaft of light from a rear window falls upon a wood-burning stove and a checkerboard set between two barrels. An invoice on the desk beside the window states that Brittain paid $14 for the stove in 1900.

"I don't think my great-grandfather ever threw away a single piece of paper," Sudderth said. "We have five washtubs of invoices and paperwork."

Like her father, Verdie Ledford was a pack rat for posterity. Inside Ledford's 122-year-old house, Sudderth and his wife found old feed and flour sacks that had been washed and neatly folded inside a wardrobe closet. The sacks now line the walls of the store's second floor, where Sudderth has assembled a stable of old farm implements and hand tools.

Brittain's store is a remarkable place made of ordinary things. It is a simple shrine to the past and a family who didn't believe in throwing things away.

"We like it to be just as it was," said Sudderth's wife, Pat. "We're just not ones for change."

July 9, 1990

One House: Mental Illness

Over the years, the neighbors watched the 1922 College Park bungalow deteriorate and, with it, the sanity of the woman who lived inside.

A small, thin, blonde in her 40s, she was the only child of wealthy parents who bought her the house on a street of middle-class homes in 2002.

At first, she seemed to fit in well: a woman of intelligence, style and class.

Later, she just seemed eccentric.

Eventually, she became the neighbor from hell.

She hung an ice skate beside the front door that was wired to the lighting fixture so that anyone who touched it would get a shock. She bathed in a garbage can. She parked her car on her front yard, doors open, music blaring, draped with clothing. She became belligerent to the point that her next-door neighbor feared for his wife and child.

From 2005 to 2012, Orlando police were called to her house 139 times, often by neighbors who complained of everything from bizarre behavior to the condition of the house that was becoming a blight. The front porch was cluttered with clothes, furniture and appliances. Her front lawn came to look like a perpetual, chaotic yard sale.

Code enforcement was called to her house by neighbors 36 times. Entering the home, they found it piled so high with garbage, clothing and household debris that they condemned it as unfit for human habitation. She would clean up the house enough to make it livable.

Her relationship with the neighbors became poisonous and hostile. The house and yard filled again with junk and garbage. The cycle kept spinning -- complaints, reports, citations -- like an endless loop of madness.

Living in Garbage

Orlando police Capt. Robert Anzeuto was in his car when

the call came over the radio about someone driving backward at a high speed down a residential street. As soon as he heard the address, he knew who it was.

Anzeuto knocked on the door and called her name. He knocked some more. Then he looked between the curtains into the living room. What he saw was a mound of trash, clothing and garbage. Then the mound moved. He saw the woman, unclothed, emerge from the trash heap.

He told her to get dressed and come outside. They needed to talk.

Until this point, over all those years, all those calls, all those visits, Orlando police had never been able to take the woman into custody under the Baker Act and get her into treatment.

The criteria are simple: Is the person a danger herself or others or incapable of taking care of herself? The woman was always too composed, too rational, too smart to meet the test.

But now she was crawling from beneath a mound of garbage inside her house.

Anzeuto called Lt. Sue Brown, who headed the Police Department's team of officers trained to deal with the mentally ill. When Brown arrived, she called Laura Gailey, who managed the Central Receiving Center, where people who are Baker Acted are taken.

Gailey said she would be right over. This is not normal procedure. Mental-health professionals do not make house calls. But Gailey knew Brown through their work together in the Crisis Intervention Training program that taught police officers how to deal with the mentally ill.

When Gailey arrived, nothing the woman said or the way she presented herself met the criteria of the Baker Act. Gailey needed to see inside the house.

Another officer, Phil Peet, who had established a rapport with the woman, told her they couldn't leave until they looked inside her house. She opened the door. There was a narrow passage through the piles of trash that led to a kitchen with the mess and disorder of a garbage dump. There was a pillow in the dishwasher, a book inside the stove. In the living room, a fur stole hung from a ceiling light fixture.

Laura Gailey had seen enough. She signed the Baker Act papers to bring the woman in for treatment. But the woman had three dachshunds she said she couldn't leave behind. Brown left and came back with a crate, dog food and the promise she would take the dogs to Pet Rescue by Judy.

The woman slid into the police car that would take her to the Central Receiving Center at Lakeside. Within 72 hours, she would be eligible for release.

A Broken Mind

Mike Rhodes has been here before. His job, as head of Orlando Code Enforcement, is lined with people who live in homes overrun with dogs and cats, convert their houses into warehouses for hoarding, turn their front lawns into junkyards.

The task of code enforcement is to ensure the ordinances of orderliness are enforced -- not to determine whether those violations are the manifestations of mental illness. But Rhodes knew the woman in the 1922 bungalow and understood that sticking within the limits of code enforcement wouldn't solve the problem for her or the people who lived on her street.

He also knew that condemnation didn't work. Condemning the homes of the mentally ill creates mentally ill homeless people.

She had the money to clean the place up and move back in.

Something more had to be done.

The woman's parents are dead, so Rhodes and Anzeuto set up a meeting with the trustees who managed the woman's money and convinced them that while she was undergoing treatment at Lakeside, and her house was under condemnation once again, that they should find her the help she needs.

Their argument was pretty simple: If she had a broken arm, would you be responsible for her medical care? Yes. Well, this woman has a broken mind.

The trustees arranged for the woman to receive mental-health treatment following her release from Lakeside. In July 2012, a judge ruled her mentally incompetent and assigned her a guardian. After the home was cleaned out, the guardian arranged for its sale. In October 2013, a new owner bought the property for

$352,000.

The mentally ill woman who once lived there is in a treatment facility.

Today, the house blends in with the rest of the neighborhood, a classy Craftsman-style bungalow with potted plants, lamps and stylish patio furniture on the front porch.

The neighbors have their street back.

This house could be in any neighborhood. Mental illness affects the community on all levels: neighbors, police, code enforcement, mental-health providers, the courts. But working independently, residents can only complain, police can only arrest, inspectors can only condemn, mental-health counselors can only treat and release.

When agencies help residents by working together, solutions happen.

"We all had to change the way we were looking at it," Rhodes said. "Here we needed to take a different approach."

Because doing the same thing over and over and expecting a different result is the definition of insanity.

December 19, 2014

AGE

Old People: Introduction

At 9 a.m., the Westminster Towers shuttle bus pulls in front of the Publix supermarket on Orange Avenue, unloading 11 old women and one old man.

This time of day, most of the customers in the grocery store are old people. As they push their shopping carts up and down the bakery and produce aisles, nobody pays much attention to them. Nobody cares that Kay Jackson, 82, uses her shopping cart for balance like a walker with wheels. Or notices how 83-year-old Jack Goldman pushes his cart with a portable oxygen tank nestled in the kiddie seat.

Nobody sees them because old people are invisible.

They disappear from TV screens and movies, magazine covers, ads and commercials as if a whole generation gets air-brushed away when its hair turns white. In our culture, longevity means outliving yourself as a target audience.

It's not just the media that erase old people from view. Fading eyesight, and fear, remove them from the sidewalks and roads after dark. Some of them hide themselves in communities that ban anyone under the age of 55. Others eat early-bird specials to avoid the crowds and the kids. And as individuals, we edit them out of our personal perceptions. If we notice old people at all, we see stereotypes -- the gray heads, the stooped postures, the stiff steps, the wrinkled skin.

We see them as two-dimensional obstacles -- getting in our way, walking or driving too slowly. But maybe there's a reason we don't look beyond those stereotypes: Old people are embodiments of time -- both past and future.

We tune them out because they are messengers from the past, a world long gone. And we fear them because they are like Dorian Gray mirrors of our future selves. Old people reflect the inevitable alterations to the mind and body caused by time. It's an image abhorrent to Americans who spend $10 billion annually on face lifts, cosmetic surgery, hair implants and Rogaine just to erase the surface effects of aging.

So we tend to look away, ignore and dismiss old people. We cheat ourselves by pretending that they have no relevance to our lives, denying the reality that most of what we encounter has already been experienced by those who passed through time ahead of us.

It has been said that the death of an old person is like the burning of a library. If so, Westminster Towers in Orlando is a library building 19 stories tall. Inside that building live 396 residents whose cumulative existence totals 33,907 years of life. It is but one retirement high-rise in Central Florida, where 275,000 residents over the age of 70 total 21 million years of life.

Florida, home to a higher percentage of the elderly than anywhere in the nation, is the Library of Congress of old people. There are 2 million Floridians over the age of 70 with 157 million years of life on Earth. Locked within those years is an archive of knowledge, experience, achievement and heartbreak. In Florida's high-rises, retirement communities, and neighborhoods are men and women who knew the heights of fame, the lows of loss, the extraordinary triumphs and everyday disappointments of a long life.

Every hour, 14 of them die in Florida, taking with them the stories of their lives and a living piece of our collective past. Some are libraries of unread books. Others are the bestsellers of their generation. Within the past 16 months, baseball great Joe DiMaggio died at home in Hollywood, Fla.; actress Hedy Lamarr died in her Casselberry home; book editor Clifton Fadiman died on Sanibel Island; actor Durward Kirby died in a nursing home in Fort Myers; and Thomas W. Ferebee, the man who dropped the bomb on Hiroshima, died at home in Windermere.

Longevity is the great leveler of life. It makes neighbors of the mighty and the ordinary, the strong and the frail, the brilliant and the demented. Judging only by the color of the hair and the wrinkles of the skin, you can't tell Who? from Who's Who.

You don't know that the old white man behind the wheel of a big white Cadillac was the CEO of General Motors in the 1960s. Or the small gray-haired woman tutoring students at Jones High School was a university president in New York in the 1970s. Or the older black man picking up his great-granddaughter at preschool is a renowned jazz composer.

Perhaps by considering the old age of remarkable people

like them, we can see beyond stereotypes to the essential humanity of all old people.

At Westminster Towers, there are inventors, artists, housewives, judges, salesmen, clerks, musicians, businessmen, singers, legislators, saxophone players, writers, ministers, nurses and hairdressers. You can't tell just by appearances which of those old people pushing their shopping carts through the Publix worked 30 years for the Pentagon, or was a professional singer, or owned a chain of photography stores, or ran the switchboard at Westminster Towers when it first opened in 1975.

After shopping, they load their groceries into the back of the shuttle bus and return to the retirement high-rise where, separated and segregated from the rest of us, they disappear from view.

But today, you have a chance to open your eyes to the living repositories of time we call old people. Turn the page. Maybe in their lives you'll discover something about your own.

July 16, 2000

Old People: Muscle

We are so phobic about age that we stigmatize the word "old." Instead of describing a stage of life, old is a pejorative term, an insult. So we wrap it up in cutesy, patronizing euphemisms such as golden agers, seniors, silver hairs, late lifers. We talk to old people much like we do to children -- with a slow, singsong lilt -- but then tell ourselves we are bestowing respect when we call them senior citizens. When the elderly were truly respected they were called elders and, yes, old people.

"There are real strong reactions to calling people old in this country," says Mary Pipher, a psychologist who studies aging. "But there is nothing wrong with the word. It describes a development stage -- like a child and a teenager."

Even old people, living in a culture that glorifies the young and fears aging, define old in terms of the negative instead of the natural. In the youth-oriented secular religion that worships the body -- its bulging muscles, sensuous curves, and smooth skin -- to be old is to be an infidel.

"In life, you're inferior because you're old," says Marie St. Pierre, a former golf champion. "Your skin begins to lag, your stomach sags, and you're a pain in the ass to everyone."

St. Pierre is 89 with auburn-colored hair, a saucy sense of humor and a sexuality that didn't flame out when her body aged and she moved into an assisted-living center in Boca Raton.

"I have one deep, dark secret," St. Pierre says, leaning forward in her chair. "I'd like to have a younger lover. I mean that." She'd like a lover who is 29 because at that age, she says, "He knows how to make love, he knows when to make love. Under that, they're kind of groping in the dark."

But what St. Pierre desires even more than a young lover is to be young again herself: "I would like to be 30 forever."

The yearning for everlasting youth is universal and eternal. Egyptians decorated their tombs 3,500 years ago with formulas for immortality potions. The same 13th-century alchemists searching for ways to turn common objects into gold were also seeking the "philosopher's stone" that would remove the impurities of the body that cause a person to age. In the

1920s, Americans were eating anti-aging yogurt the way that melatonin and vitamin E tablets are consumed today.

The new millennium spin on the timeless desire to stay young is that aging is a disease. On the radio, a commercial targets people over 35 with the promise that an $80 bottle of powder will unleash a youth hormone produced by the body that enhances energy, sex drive and intellect while you sleep.

"Research has found that age is a treatable disease," the commercial says.

On bookstore shelves, thoughtful treatises on aging are squeezed into obscurity by volume after volume offering formulas for staying young: Stop Aging Now! The Anti-Aging Zone. The Anti-Aging Hormones. Age-Proofing Your Body. Live Now, Age Later.

There are many benefits to the active, healthy lifestyles advocated by those books, but anti-aging is not one of them. All those vitamins, powders and pills, those hours on the treadmill, the forsaking of ice cream and caffeine, may lead to a healthier old age, but it can't slow down, stop, and reverse the aging of the body.

The old myth is that old age leads inevitably to frailty, feebleness and senility. We know now that frailty, feebleness and senility are the products of disease, not age. The new myth is that if you eat right, exercise enough and keep your mind active, you can derail old age.

The nation's leading cell biologist, Leonard Hayflick, calls that pure hokum: "The nostrums that lifestyle and diet will slow down the aging process is a load of garbage. If they have any effect at all, they have an effect on disease not on aging."

But eliminating the diseases of old age doesn't mean we'd live forever, either. If the three leading causes of death among old people -- cancer, cardiovascular disease and stroke -- were suddenly to disappear, the average life span would increase from about 78 years to 100. That's a long way from immortality but closer to the biological longevity of human beings, which is somewhere between 115 and 120 years.

As the body ages, it loses much of its ability to repel disease. But confusing aging with disease prevents us from separating fact from myth when it comes to the changes that take place over time.

The body ages like a wacky clock shop where all the clocks are running at different speeds. There are chronological aging clocks, biological aging clocks, functional aging clocks, cognitive aging clocks. Clocks that control individual cells, skin, muscles, bones, organs, hair, brain.

The master clock of aging is encoded in the genetic makeup of the individual. Researchers think longevity is determined roughly half by the genes inherited from our ancestors and half by habits, lifestyles and the environment.

The most precise -- and least accurate -- clock is chronological aging. Chronological aging is simple math: Everyone born 80 years ago is 80 years old. It's how we tell a person's age, but it doesn't tell us much about the person.

Biological aging, on the other hand, is the calculus of aging. It explains why two 80-year-olds can look so different. The older we become, the harder it is to tell a person's age based on appearance, because the internal clocks of each individual run at different speeds. Biological aging is why we say, "You don't look 80," and doctors tell patients, "You're an 80-year-old man in a 60-year-old's body."

Although the rate of biological aging varies from person to person and from skin to bone to muscle, normal aging changes the body in predictable ways. The changes begin in the 30s, accelerate in the 40s, and start to slow down again in the 70s.

As a demonstration model for how the body ages, take Monte Irvin, 81. Inducted into the Baseball Hall of Fame, he was a star outfielder in the National Negro League and the New York Giants. He owes his success to sports, building a good life for his family with his muscles and bones. In return, sports have extracted a price from his body.

Irvin has a degenerated disc in his spine, arthritis in his back, fading eyesight and artificial knees. Two thin scars run down the middle of both knees where bone, ligaments and cartilage have been removed and replaced with metal and plastic. This meld of medicine and mechanics allows him to walk stiffly, but without pain, on his artificial knees. Whenever Monte Irvin passes through a metal detector, alarms go off.

Even without the abuse from sports, Irvin's muscles, joints and ligaments changed as he aged. His joints reached their peak flexibility around the age of 20, about the same time his cartilage began to thin and become less spongy. His muscles started to lose strength in his 40s. In the 60s and 70s, there's a 10 percent to 20 percent reduction in strength; in the 70s and 80s, a loss of 30 percent to 40 percent with a greater decline in the legs than the arms and hands.

Until he reached his 30s, Irvin's bones were in a constant state of regeneration completely rebuilding the skeletal scaffolding of his body about every seven years. One set of cells -- osteoclasts -- tears down bone matter and another set of cells -- osteoblasts -- replaces it. Bone density reaches its peak around the age of 18. By 35, the osteoblasts fall behind the osteoclasts, and the bones start losing mass at the rate of about 1 percent a year. Since estrogen stimulates the bone-building osteoblasts, women experience an acceleration of bone loss as they go though menopause. Generally, men lose about 17 percent of the bone mass and women about 20 percent as they age.

Changes in bone and muscle also result in a decrease in height. Women, on average, shrink 2 inches; men, 1.25 inches. Osteoporosis -- a disease that afflicts about 10 million old people -- causes the vertebrae of the spine to compress. When the 12 thoracic vertebrae break down, it causes the hunchback known as the "dowager's hump." Severe osteoporosis can cause old people to lose between 5 and 8 inches in height. Osteoporosis is also a leading contributor to hip fractures, which send 300,000 old people to the hospital every year.

Changes to the skin are the most superficial, and dreaded, aspect of aging. Dermatologist Albert Kligman once observed: "Everyone wants to live a long life, but no one wants to look old."

Skin is composed of three layers: the epidermis, dermis and hypodermis, each of which changes with age.

The top layer, the epidermis, is constantly replacing dead cells. By age 70, the body has shed more than 40 pounds of skin.

But as we age, the rate of cells' being lost exceeds that of their replacement. The epidermis becomes thinner, making it susceptible to wrinkling. Beneath the epidermis, the dermis also thins with the loss of the protein collagen and elastin fibers, which make the skin less flexible. The hypodermis, containing fat that helps regulate body temperature, also thins with age. Old people typically feel comfortable at temperatures 10 to 15 degrees warmer than young people -- hence the popularity of Florida.

The 3 million sweat glands on the body also begin to disappear or stop functioning with age, providing one of the benefits of growing old: less body odor.

Elsewhere throughout Monte Irvin's body, changes are taking place. By 70, the efficiency of his lungs has been reduced by half. His kidneys started to shrink around age 30. By age 90, the kidneys have lost half of their filtering capacities.

Despite his physical problems, Monte Irvin hasn't surrendered his old age to his ailments. He still works out every day on an ancient exercise bike that has followed him around for 48 years and a treadmill wedged into the corner of his garage. For his back, he does calisthenics three times a day.

"My father died at 87. I'm trying at least to get to his age," Irvin says. "I don't know if I'm going to make it."

When separated from disease, the normal aging of the body results in a gradual, continual loss of strength, stamina and agility. Despite the image of old age as a time of wheelchairs and dementia, only 4 percent of the population over 65 resides in nursing homes.

Nothing can stop the aging process, but better nutrition, exercise, and the elimination of disease do produce more physically fit old people. By the end of the 20th century, swimmers in their 50s and 60s were turning in times that won Olympic medals in the early part of the century by athletes in their teens and 20s.

At 18, Eleanor Holm was the fastest woman swimmer in the world, winning a gold medal at the 1932 Olympics for the 100-meter backstroke. An Olympic swimmer since the age of 14, Holm later went on to star in the Aquacade of the 1939 New York World's Fair -- performing so many shows that her hair turned green from the chlorine. Now 86, Holm is recovering from a broken hip that prevents her from playing golf or tennis.

"I should swim. I know it would help my hip. But it's so boring," Holm says. "Many times, I'll get in a bathing suit and go down to the pool and put my foot in the water and say, `Eleanor, you don't have to do this anymore'."

Treatment of disease, coupled with healthier lifestyles, holds the promise of old age as a time when the body may move slower and less efficiently but without feebleness and frailty. Among gerontologists, this is called "successful aging" or "optimal aging."

Optimal aging takes the usual lifecycle arc of ascent, peak, and long, slow decline and turns it into a rectangle with old age as a long plateau that ends with a short quick drop at death. It's one of those new discoveries that has been around as long as today's *old people* who are competing in marathons, parachuting out of airplanes, downhill skiing, even returning to space.

Staying in shape is what gets Farris Bryant up in the morning three days a week to become the first one inside the door at the Jacksonville Yacht Club exercise room at 5:30 a.m. He spends an hour working on weight machines and an exercise bike.

Bryant, a former governor of Florida, is 85. Longevity is not his goal: "My doctors say that in my shape, I could live to be 100. Who wants to do that? Every day is just another day of being old."

Bryant exercises to keep his body from betraying him, falling into disuse and frailty. He wants to maintain his physical self for as long as he can and shorten his decline before death -- the new trajectory of optimal aging.

But even with successful aging, most people will spend the end of their lives fighting a fatal disease. Hayflick describes optimal aging as dodging life's bullets -- the accidents, diseases, illnesses, assaults and miscellaneous mayhems that interrupt our quest for immortality.

"The people who talk about successful aging are talking about people who got lucky. We don't understand why they are lucky," Hayflick contends. "After you get past 80, you have dodged the most well-aimed bullets and now have fewer bullets being fired. You have to get lucky dodging bullets."

Old people adjust their lives to bodies with less elasticity in the skin, less density in the bones, less strength in the muscles, less oxygen in the blood. Some monitor their aches and ailments like others watch The Weather Channel and compare their surgeries like cooks trading recipes.

Mary R. Peterson is 88. She has arthritis in her knees, an artificial joint in her left thumb and is undergoing chemotherapy following surgery for ovarian cancer. Riding a bike is her therapy. Raised too poor to own a bike as a child, she bought her first bicycle when she retired at 73. Bike riding reduces her pain, says Peterson, who lives in a Volusia retirement community.

Pain is a common companion to old age. Nearly 80 percent of people over the age of 70 endure at least one chronic illness. More than half have arthritis, a third have hypertension, a fourth have heart disease. Pain-free old people boast of not taking drugs like young people brag about the drugs they've tried.Peterson makes a distinction between the condition of her body and the state of her mind: "Pain is inevitable. Misery is optional. I refuse to be miserable."

In separating aging from disease, we must also separate what the aging body feels from what the aging mind thinks about growing old.

"Old age is not a disease," Gray Panthers founder Maggie Kuhn once said. "It is strength and survivorship, triumph over all kinds of vicissitudes and disappointments, trials and illnesses."

In old age, it is mind that compensates for muscle's failure.

July 16, 2000

Old People: Mind

Music is life's elixir. It's time conveyed by a tune, memories encoded in melodies.

It shows in the eyes of the old people dancing to the songs of their youth at the Polish American Club of Vero Beach in a hall with the lights turned low and a four-piece band, The Tempos, on the stage. The men are dressed in suits, plaid or checked sports coats, turquoise slacks, vests, suspenders, white belts and matching shoes, turtlenecks and gold chains. Eyeglass cases protrude from dress-shirt breast pockets. The women wear long floral dresses, gold shoes, polka-dot skirts and jewelry on their wrists that catch spots of light from the mirrored ball spinning overhead.

Everybody in Goreczny Hall is old. But the way they hold each other as they flow counterclockwise around the dance floor makes them ageless. There is grace in their movements, sophistication in their footwork, serenity on their faces.

It's a wondrous thing to witness, men and women moving together with the kind of effortless synchronization that comes from time and repetition. Their skin is lined with the years. Their hair is gray and white. But they dance as if they were young again.

Eighty-seven-year-old Joseph H. Burckhalter is in the middle of the dance floor in the arms of his wife, Julia. His dancing is stiff, his movement mechanical. He has osteoporosis, one kidney, a bad left lung, heart problems and a ringing in his ears that hasn't stopped since he caught malaria at age 14.

But within that failing body is a mind of a scientist who still works on theories about the origin of life, ideas about the causes of mental illness, proposals for an institute for medicinal chemistry.

"I have a folder of ideas I want to pursue," Burckhalter says. "I have things I want to do."

Old age is seen as perpetual decline with mind and body riding the downward slope in tandem. It's not true. Research has rebuked the idea of an "unsound body, unsound mind." The breakdown of the physical does not automatically drag down the mental.

Old people confined to wheelchairs, who have suffered from debilitating diseases such as cancer, diabetes, hypertension and even stroke, can still be mentally sharp. Similarly, research has shown that keeping physically fit is no guarantee a person will remain mentally vigorous in old age. The brain has a mind of its own, and the diseases of the brain strike the physically fit as well as the brilliant.

Urico Rossi was a musical virtuoso who attended Juilliard, Eastman and Yale as a classical violinist. From 1947 to 1979, he was a member of the Berkshire String Quartet, a renowned chamber quartet. He was handsome, stylish, charming, charismatic and as skilled in romance as music. In 1944, when he was 28, Rossi met Hazel, an attractive 18-year-old from South Carolina.

"He wooed me with all these lovely things. He sent me roses all the time and books of poetry. He took me out to wonderful places for dinner. He just bowled me over," says Hazel Rossi. "And when he played the violin, it just touched my heart, it was so beautiful."

Today, Urico Rossi is 83, suffers from Alzheimer's disease and resides in Village Oaks, a Winter Springs assisted-living center. He has forgotten how to play the violin and can't remember Hazel's name. The disease of his mind eliminates memory as quickly as it forms, like raindrops turning to steam on hot summer pavement. To Hazel, it erases her as well: "It makes me so sad that he can't remember me. It just negates my existence."

Alzheimer's, discovered in 1906, is the new word for senility. What was once presumed to be the inevitable consequence of old age is now known to be a disease that eats away the brain with tangles of fibers and growths called plaques. Although the cause of Alzheimer's is unknown, the odds increase with age. At ages 65-70, it afflicts 2 percent of the population. Over 85, it afflicts more than 20 percent.

Across town, Myrtle Bridges is 102 years old and lives on the ninth floor of Lutheran Towers retirement high-rise in Orlando.

She was born on a farm in Iowa, gave piano lessons at 15, married a hardware salesman, loved to listen to classical music on her record player and enjoyed going to the theater.

Her life was not without tragedy or illness. Her husband died from hypertension at 69. One son died at 62 from cancer that rendered him unrecognizable to his mother: "He was just like an old man."

Myrtle Bridges' mind is as flawless as Rossi's is fractured. She remembers names, dates and experiences from a life that spans more than a century, including a vacation with her husband's cranky mother through the Black Hills in a hot summer thick with grasshoppers: "We never took my mother-in-law again."

She still reads and manages her own finances, buying and selling stocks. She is one of those optimal agers whose mind has dodged more bullets than the Lone Ranger: "You know, I'm very lucky. I can tell a little joke, and I can get up and take care of myself. I don't know why I was chosen."

Rossi and Bridges are opposite extremes on the spectrum of aging and the brain. Rossi represents the brain affected by disease. Bridges' is the brain as it ages naturally. Rossi, whose father also had dementia, may have hastened the development of his Alzheimer's with heavy drinking. Bridges may have forestalled any mental decline by avoiding cigarettes, alcohol and caffeine.

But researchers have found that the brains of even mentally sharp old people such as Myrtle Bridges often have the same characteristic plaques and tangles -- albeit far fewer -- in their brains as those with Alzheimer's. This leads scientists to think the brain has a reserve capacity for memory and intellect even late in life that compensates or replaces areas affected by aging.

Unlike muscle, bone and skin, the brain's cells -- called neurons -- do not divide. The adult brain, weighing about 3 pounds, has about the same 15 billion neurons as it did in infancy. The latest research suggests new brain cells may be born in adulthood, but scientists don't know if it occurs in old age.

Although neurons do not multiply, they do grow in size as

we age. And the branchlike tentacles called dendrites, through which neurons communicate, increase in number and length as we grow older. The more mental stimulation the brain receives, the longer and more prolific the dendrites become -- regardless of age.

The ability of the brain to adapt with age compensates for its shrinking and loss of brain cells over time. After age 30, the brain loses an estimated 100,000 brain cells a day. The loss of neurons causes the brain to shrink as we grow older. The brain of a 90-year-old weighs about 10 percent less than the brain of a 20-year-old.

Within the brain, the hippocampus -- a critical area of memory and learning -- starts dying at age 30. By old age, nearly a third of the hippocampus neurons are lost.

The cerebellum, which affects our sense of balance, coordination, posture and other motor function, begins to lose mass around age 60. In old age, the cerebellum is 25 percent smaller than it was in youth.

Yet at the same time brain cells are dying and the brain is shrinking, it is also gaining more knowledge. Even with the hippocampus shedding neurons, researchers have found that a 60-year-old brain contains four times the information of a 20-year-old brain. Learning is not an activity confined by the size of the brain or the age of the person.

Stanley Ward was 81 when he finished high school. Ward is a big man who wears suspenders and his white hair cut close to the scalp. His voice is hickory-smoked from growing up on a farm in east Tennessee. His father never went to school. His mother, with a fourth-grade education, held a special status in the community: She was the one folks came to when they needed a letter written or read.

Stanley Ward was an excellent student but never made it past eighth grade, when the Depression cut his education short.

"In 19 and 30 I had to quit school to help my daddy," says Ward, 85, who lives in Longwood Retirement Village nursing home. "We didn't have any money. There wasn't any money anywhere anyhow."

He found a job that paid $18.20 for a 52-hour week in a

factory that made rayon out of wood pulp and Karo syrup and worked in that factory until retiring in 1958.

Ward has always had intelligence, and the unfinished business of his education nagged him like a song without a chorus. In 1996, under a self-study program at Seminole Community College, he finished high school 66 years after dropping out.

Stanley Ward's case shows that the cognitive aging of his mind runs on a different clock than biological aging of his body that has suffered from a stroke, stomach ulcers, back surgery, five heart operations, lung and prostate cancer and poor circulation that makes walking painful.

Learning doesn't stop as a person grows older, but just using your mind can't prevent cognitive decline. The old adage of "use it or lose it" is as much a myth as "old dogs can't learn new tricks." Studies conducted by Harvard researcher Douglas Powell found declines even in old people who remained mentally stimulated: "Cognitive decline, like physical decline, is a normal event in everyone's life."

Yet just as remaining physically fit can forestall the onset of disease, staying mentally sharp can slow mental losses as we age. Reading books, doing crossword puzzles and challenging the mind are like pouring fertilizer on the forest of neurons in the brain, says Earl Zimmerman, an expert on aging and the brain: "The brain gets rid of the old trees, but the remaining trees send out new branches."

Memory resides inside the brain in many different forms. Disease affects all forms of memory, but age erodes some types of memory more than others.

There are times when the mind reaches out for something familiar and grasps only air. Gone is a name, a date, a phone number, a street address. While it can be caused by stress, fatigue, drugs, alcohol and medications, we often take it as the sure sign of aging. We even call it a "senior moment."

But that type of memory -- verbal memory -- is not the first sign of old age. Before we start to draw memory blanks, the way our brain processes information begins to slow; the ability to do two things at once (dual-task attention) starts to slide; and the brain's capacity to hold information in the mind while using it to solve a problem (working memory) decreases. The sharpest decline, which begins in the 40s, comes in the spatial memory that helps us remember where we parked the car at the mall or left our eyeglasses and car keys.

Oddly enough, at the same time that our verbal memory makes it more difficult to recall specific words, our ability to remember more words -- our vocabulary -- increases with age.

Some other forms of memory do not diminish with age. Autobiographical memory -- our ability to recall the events of our lives -- does not decline with age absent of disease. Researchers have found ways of triggering long-forgotten memories with electronic stimulation to the brain, leading to the belief that the memories don't disappear, but the retrieval mechanisms of the brain fail and malfunction.

Semantic memory -- our knowledge about the world -- tends to increase with age. Perspective memory -- remembering to do something in the future -- declines with age.

But the mind is much more than a spongy mass of neurons and memories. It is also the lens through which a person views the world based on the past. Today's old people grew up in a world fundamentally different from the one they now occupy. And that difference distinguishes them, and their perceptions of the world, from that of their children, grandchildren and great-grandchildren.

Before 1900, the experiences of one generation were not significantly different from the lives of older generations. Jimmy Carter recalled growing up on a family farm that didn't have electricity or indoor plumbing until he was 14: "Rosalynn and I grew up in southwest Georgia, and our early lifestyle was more like that of our distant ancestors than that of our grandchildren."

Jimmy and Rosalynn Carter, and their generation, were raised in a time when manners mattered. In a small town such as Plains, Ga., where everyone knew his or her neighbors, rudeness and insults could turn into resentments and grudges that lasted lifetimes. In Plains during the Depression, manners and dignity were sometimes all a family had.

Raised in a place and a time that no longer exist, old

people find themselves estranged from an urban society in which attitude supplants manners, humility is outdated and arrogance is hip.

The world of polite children, thrifty saving accounts and small-town familiarity has largely disappeared but still exists inside the minds of old people, just as music from their youth still plays in their ears. Old people recreate their lost worlds in retirement communities that exclude children and adults under 55, and in Polish-American dance halls, and with old-time big bands such as the Escorts that play nursing homes and senior centers.

"Older people gravitate toward each other. We can talk about the same things. We speak the same language," says George E. Skeet, 72, who plays the saxophone with the Escorts. "My passion is big bands, but I can't talk to 20-year-olds about big bands. To them, a big band is five guitars."

There may be a tendency among old people to live in the past, a place that makes more sense than today's world. But as the world changed, so did they. The brains of 2-year-olds and 20-year-olds have more neurons than the brains of 70-year-olds and 80-year-olds but lack the perspective on life that comes only with age.

With old age, which adds experience to intellect, comes meaning.

July 16, 2000

Old People: Meaning

If older meant wiser, con men wouldn't be scamming old people out of their life savings and shysters wouldn't get away with charging widows a fortune to privacy-proof their homes, fix phony Freon leaks or repair major appliances.

H.L. Mencken sounded like a guy who had just watched the rain wash away his new asphalt driveway when he said, "The older I grow, the more I distrust the familiar doctrine that age brings wisdom."

In earlier cultures, the old were revered for their wisdom. But in modern society, it's the attributes of youth -- strength, beauty and vigor -- that matter more.

"This country values energy more than wisdom," says Bob Kurland, 75, an All-America basketball player who finds younger generations unreceptive to the lessons learned by older people. "People have to want to listen."

But a long life by itself does not beget wisdom any more than wealth bestows class. Wisdom comes from how we deal with adversity, learn from experience and come to understand ourselves.

There are old people for whom life's crises bestow bitterness and resentment, who blame others for their misfortunes, who keep making foolish mistakes over and over and who have no more personal insight than they did when they were teenagers. They lack the disposition for wisdom.

Researchers have found that as we age our bodies change, but our personalities remain essentially unchanged. We don't naturally mellow with age or become grumpier with time.

So some people have a stronger inclination than others toward wisdom in old age. Wisdom, in essence, is the search for the meaning in life. Some people feel compelled to explore the significance of life, and they become our sages, educators, artists, poets, songwriters, philosophers, religious leaders, writers and, quite often, our grandparents.

University of Florida researcher Monika Ardelt studied wisdom in older people. Wise people seemed to have an ability to see beneath the surface of events, view things from different perspectives and feel compassion for other people: "You have to understand the deeper meanings of life. Everybody knows we are going to die, but to really understand what it means is wisdom."

Jacqueline Grennan Wexler learned the meaning of death early in life when her older brother, Jack, died. In his death, she understood her own mortality at an age when most adolescents think they are invincible: "I was 15 years old when this brother I worshipped died at 21. That had an enormous effect on me. I've always known life was going to be over."

After her brother's death, she became a nun, changing her birth name, Jean Marie, to Jacqueline in his honor. Her life, from then on, became dedicated to making a difference in the world, and she did that by demonstrating kindness, self-control, modesty and dispassion -- traits identified by Harvard researcher Douglas Powell as elements of wisdom.

In the 1960s, as "Sister J," she became nationally known as the dynamo fund-raiser of Webster College in St. Louis. In the 1970s, as president of Hunter College in New York, she kept the university running while New York City was going bankrupt and college campuses were being shut down by anti-war protests. In the 1980s, she ran the National Conference of Christians and Jews. In 2000, she tutors students who need help with algebra.

"Wisdom is gaining esteem for yourself and other people at the same time that you are gaining a greater sense of humor," she says.

While time alone cannot create wisdom, it is the long, slow simmering of age that brings the ingredients to a boil. Old age allows people the time and opportunity to think and reflect -- what gerontologists call "aging and sage-ing."

There is freedom in old age to do what you want, say what you like, wear black knee socks with plaid shorts if you wish, and eat supper at 4 in the afternoon if you want. There is liberation in old age for people who were reared in teamwork, cooperation and keeping your feelings to yourself.

The common perception of old age is that it's a place populated by people who are stuck in a rut, resistant to change, inflexible and stubborn. Some people are. There is comfort in routine.

But old age is also freedom to change. It's the last chance to resolve family feuds and grudges -- and there is wisdom in that. It's the privilege to try something new with the experience to know that failure isn't fatal, and the opportunity to be creative in ways not possible while raising a family or building a career.

There are two types of creativity, and both flourish among old people. One is the creativity that changes or influences society as a whole. It's Frank Lloyd Wright designing the Guggenheim Museum in New York at 91; Helen Keller writing about Ann Sullivan, her miracle worker, at 75; Pablo Picasso painting "Rape of the Sabines" at 81. It's also Nelson Mandela becoming South Africa's president at 75; Mahatma Gandhi winning India's independence at 77; Alan Greenspan manipulating the economy at 74.

Harvard professor Howard Gardner calls this creativity with a "Big C."

But there is also creativity with a "little c" that manifests itself in the smaller, more personal ways that people change. It shows up in the ordinary lives of everyday people who, regardless of age, develop new skills, find new ways to do things, create new approaches to old problems.

"The definition of creativity is bringing something new into existence that is valued. A new recipe, a floral arrangement, a garden, is valued by those who benefit from it," says Gene D. Cohen, a psychiatrist who has studied aging and creativity.

Among old people, "little c" creativity often sprouts from loss and adversity. It's found in the hands of Edward Hoag, an 80-year-old woodcarver who lives in the Stanford Centre assisted-living facility in Altamonte Springs. Hoag is legally blind, and his hands have become his eyes. He carves by holding a rectangular piece of 2-by-4 scrap wood in his hands, feeling the texture of the wood grain and the shape of an animal slowly coaxed out by his whittling knife: an owl, a pelican, a squirrel, a jackrabbit.

His carvings are smaller, simpler, more basic than the intricate wood eagles he created in his younger days while working as a steel mill supervisor. But it keeps Hoag occupied in a world that grows dimmer all the time, and it distracts his mind from the death of his wife of 56 years.

Hoag relies upon his wood carving for entertainment, satisfaction and meaning in old age: "I'm just glad I have something to keep me occupied. Most of the people here don't have much to do."

Edward Hoag's creativity fills voids left by the loss of his wife and his eyesight. Loss is death in increments. In old age, it's the loss of vision, bone and muscle mass, hair, hearing, agility, sense of balance, coordination. The loss of spouses, friends, family members, classmates, co-workers and children. The loss of drivers licenses, mobility, autonomy, independence and freedom. The loss of memory and mental acuity. The loss of work, income and identity.

Without the ability to recreate themselves in old age, to exercise "little c" creativity, some people become lost in their own lives after they retire. After a lifetime of being defined by what they do for a living, doing nothing means they become nothing.

It's the way that people deal with loss in old age that leads to both wisdom and creativity.

Georgia Solomon is 80 years old and lives in Westminster Towers in Orlando. She taught home economics, outlived three husbands, raised two sons, and played the violin since the age of 8. She still gets a thrill just listening to the strings section of a symphony orchestra: "It's so exhilarating and inspiring I can hardly stand it. I'm sure it's the same high people get skiing down a mountain."

So it was a tremendous loss for Solomon when osteoarthritis made it impossible for her to play the violin anymore. Every day she awakens to pain in her hands, elbows, shoulders, hips and feet. Worse than the pain was her inability to play the violin: "I couldn't stand to hear myself practice. When I quit, I went into mourning. I was so depressed about the whole thing."

Solomon's third husband was a wise man. For Christmas, he gave her painting lessons. She's been painting now for 30 years, often while listening to classical music. Her room is filled with landscapes and her own reproductions of van Gogh paintings, which she sometimes hangs together on a wall like her own gallery of imitation masterpieces.

"I'm never going to be a Picasso. I'm never going to be someone the world will remember. But I'm not ashamed of anything I do," she says.

Creativity in old age conforms to stages we pass through in the second half of life. Gene Cohen has identified four developmental stages of aging: reevaluation, liberation, summation and encore.

Reevaluation typically begins in the 50s with a desire to find more meaning in life. Just making a living isn't good enough anymore. From many a "midlife crisis" come wisdom and creativity.

Around their 60s and the 70s, people enter a liberation phase. Retirement offers freedom at an age when people are still physically energetic and mentally active. There's a sense of "now or never" that encourages older people to try different things and revisit past interests.

From the 70s on, people enter what Cohen describes as the summing-up phase of life. Acting on the desire to leave behind a legacy, older people at this stage become benefactors, philanthropists, storytellers, autobiographers, volunteers and community activists.

By the encore phase -- 80s and beyond -- creativity takes the form of completing unfinished business and securing your place within family and community. Spirituality becomes more important in the encore phase. Mary Pipher, the psychologist, describes this stage of life as when "resilient old people have used their hardships to grow souls."

Old age provides a higher platform from which to evaluate life -- time becomes more precious than money, health more important than possessions, love more enduring than fame. Wise and creative older people do not look back and bemoan the past. Young people may never want to grow old, but not all old people desire to be young again.

"No wise man ever wished to be younger," said Jonathan Swift 300 years ago.

The old understand society's obsession with youth. They

were all young once themselves. Many would gladly trade the aches, pains and disabilities of old age for the vigor and luster of youth. But they also want younger generations to know that old age is not necessarily a ghetto of regrets and depression.

The old also advise the young to be cautious what they wish for -- including longevity. You can spend all your time and money on anti-aging books, pills, and potions and still end up alone, ill and old. Lives that outlast savings, loved ones, and health are old-age purgatories of poverty, grief and pain.

Peg Kern lives in a one-room Westminster Towers apartment stocked with the dark antique furniture from her beloved two-story stone and clapboard house in Baltimore. She misses that house and the kitchen where she cooked stuffed baked pork chops, fried chicken and lima beans. Ten years ago, her family persuaded her to sell the house and move to Westminster. "This isn't an apartment," she says. "This is a room with a bed."

Kern is 94 years old and dresses like a flower bed in comfortable, colorful clothing. Her cheeks are rouged, and her wrists heavy with bracelets. Her feet wear fuzzy pink slippers. In her youth, Kern wore a top-hat-and-tails costume as she sang for 25 years on the stage between acts of a vaudeville melodrama. When the big bands came to Baltimore and wanted a local singer, they always asked for Peg Kern.

In 1923, she married a man who worked for Maryland's highway department. She loved to sing, and he loved to listen. They lived in that big Baltimore house until his death from a heart attack at 71.

Living alone for the past 27 years, Kern spends her old age crocheting and reading biographies until 1 or 2 in the morning, long after other residents have turned off the lights: "Everybody here goes to bed at 8 o'clock."

But the attrition of a long life extracts its toll. A room with a bed is not a house. Institutional food is not home cooking. A good book is no substitute for a good husband.

"My only trouble is I have lived too long," Peg Kern says. "I'm afraid I'm going to live forever."

Kern lives in her apartment with her antique furniture and

memories of a life on stage and a husband she loved. In old age, meaning is enmeshed in memories.

When the memories go, identity is lost.

July 16, 2000

Old People: Memory

We spend lifetimes collecting, and collecting, and collecting. In the end, life reduces us to recollection. We become what we remember.

Old people are invisible to others when nobody listens to their stories, shares their lives, sees their humanity. But they can become invisible even to themselves when they outlive their ability to remember.

Five Orlando women, all born in 1900, have each collected a century of remembrances. Today, to varying degrees, they are fainter versions of their earlier selves. Chunks of their lives are missing from their minds.

Of the five, Pearl Davis has the most complete memory. It is like a flickering movie with some scratches on the surface and scenes edited out where the film broke and was spliced back together poorly.

"I was born in Sylvester, Ga. My daddy was a brick mason. He built mostly brick chimneys. My mom took care of the kids and did laundry for white people," she says.

Davis was the second youngest of eight children -- six girls and two boys. She wanted to learn music and become a teacher but never went beyond fifth grade -- just long enough to learn to read and write. She picked cotton and worked as a maid, just like her mother.

She became pregnant when she was 18 by a man who promised to marry her.

"But he fooled me. He had a wife," she says.

Her baby was born dead.

She and a sister moved from Valdosta, Ga., where they were earning $2 to $3 a week as maids, to Orlando, where they could earn $10 to $15 a week. In Orlando, she met Boston Davis, a truck driver. They were married for 10 years, separated, and reconciled.

"He was as smart as he could be, but he loved other women," she says.

Davis is a rail-thin woman in a bed with white sheets pulled to her chin, her head covered by a knitted cap. Since her 30s, Pearl Davis has been blinded by glaucoma.

She has lived so long, Davis says, that she feels more like a spirit than a person. Something unseen and otherworldly is her constant companion: "I feel somebody is with me all the time, looking out for me, like Jesus. I'm about ready to go. I'm tired of this old sinful world."

Lorena Ford, also born in 1900, has a memory more splintered than Pearl Davis'. Parts of Ford's life are missing-in-action inside her head. She remembers how she adored her father but has forgotten stories she has told all her life. Married to a county extension agent, Ford was once an accomplished gardener, cultivating day lilies and judging flower shows: "I got into it in a big way. I loved it, but I can't tell you anything about it because I can't remember."

The past resides inside her mind as a family album of mislabeled snapshots.

"Sometimes she goes back and forth between my children being her children and me being her mother," says Mary Beardall, her daughter.

Ford grew up in Alabama as the indulged only daughter with three brothers born to a Presbyterian minister: "I came into life like I was born a princess." She still wears her hair cut short and dyed the rusty red color of her youth, and maintained a Southern lady's prerogative to lie about her age until longevity spelled it out in purple icing on a chocolate cake with sweet white frosting: "Happy 100th Birthday, Nanee."

A third child of 1900, Carrie Robinson, has a memory like a jigsaw puzzle. But while the pieces of her childhood form a complete picture, the pieces of her adulthood are scattered and missing.

Robinson was one of six children born on a Georgia farm who was introduced to the hard life of field work after the eighth grade: "That's all it was, that field. Pulling cotton, pulling corn. My uncles worked me to death."

Robinson's hair is as thick as mattress stuffing, pulled back off her face and tied with a ribbon. She has a large head with cliff-like cheekbones that dominate her wide face.

She married once, when she was 14. The marriage lasted eight months. "The hardest job I had was having a husband," she says. "I'm glad I don't have to do that no more."

Robinson remembers most vividly the days of her childhood playing in the yard, playing in the garden, playing in the tree, playing in the garage. She still sings the songs of her youth: Ride, Sally, ride. Wipe your weepy eyes . . . When she wasn't playing or working in the fields, she was fighting. A flash of her past illuminates her face when she talks about being a fist-flinging girl growing up hard in rural Georgia.

"I'd fight before I got to school and before I came home," Robinson says. "Yeah, I think about it sometimes. Victory was mine."

Viola Lamb remembers even less than Carrie Robinson. Her past is a toy chest with a jumble of memories tossed inside. Some are missing parts. Others are buried so deep she doesn't know they are there. And some she couldn't forget if she wanted to.

She remembers the death of her son, Curtis: "He died just like a light was burned out." Eleven months later her daughter, Pauline, died, leaving her grief-stricken and childless.

What she remembers best is her husband, Leroy. They were high school sweethearts who grew up a few blocks from each other in Madison. Leroy Lamb worked for the telephone company. He was a heavy-set, balding man who loved to fish and eat Viola's cooking. He was mowing the lawn one day while Viola was sitting on the back steps of their house watching him. It was a hot day, and Leroy was sweating. He stopped mowing, came over to Viola, sat down beside her and died of a heart attack.

"He fell dead at my doorstep," she says.

It's been 38 years and she still mourns his death, still misses his presence.

"When I go to bed at night, I feel under the covers to see if I can find him," she says.

Now, dreams are more soothing than memories for Viola Lamb. No place feels better than her bed. She has only one request, made to strangers and friends alike. It's the wish of an old woman weary for rest, uttered in the pleading, high-pitched voice of a child: "Will you put me in my bed?"

The last of the five women, Selena Brooks, has the faintest memory of all. The century of life she looks back on today is like a dark ocean dotted with small islands of recollection.

"I was born in Florida. I think it was Ocala," Brooks says, sitting in her wheelchair with a knitted blanket draped across her lap: "I've had a beautiful life because I've done so many things."

But those things, those 100 years of experiences and stories told and retold, sink beneath the surface, beyond the reach of her recall. The inability to remember frustrates and torments Selena Brooks, who prided herself as one of those people everyone turned to when they wanted a question answered, a problem solved, an argument settled: "Oh, they used to call on me for everything. Anything they asked me, I had answers for. Now you can ask me, and I don't know nothing."

She remembers she was married three times – "Three strikes and you're out." – but she can't recall the names of her husbands or how long she was married. She taps on her head, trying to knock the memories loose.

Selena Brooks, Viola Lamb, Carrie Robinson, Lorena Ford and Pearl Davis are close to disappearing now. Old age has left their bodies shrunken, shriveled and stiffened. During a century of living, their minds have lost brain cells but gained perspective. They know what it's like to cherish something and watch it slip away.

"I don't know what's up here anymore. I don't have any memory,'' Selena Brooks says. "Lord, why, why. Why is it? That's what I want to know."

In the end, old people either compensate for loss or become consumed by what they no longer possess. But do not look away from them. If you pay attention, you'll realize that old people do more than talk about the past.

From their bodies, their minds, their souls and their memories, you can hear echoes of your own future.

July 16, 2000

CULTURE

On Any Given Sunday: Checker Kings

Bernard Dudley began playing checkers on Parramore Avenue when he was 6 years old. Now 71, he has seen the neighborhood transformed, dismantled, razed and rebuilt. Gone is the drugstore where Dudley learned to play checkers on a tree stump out back. Gone is the Dixie Doodle restaurant, Sister Reed's motel, and the house on Carter Street where Bernard Dudley was born.

One thing survives: checkers.

"I've been playing checkers here for 65 years," Dudley said. "If I could choose where to die, it would be at this checkerboard."

The players are mostly old men, like himself, who bring their own boards and checkers because the spray-painted black-and-red checkerboards installed by the city in Checker Park are worn down to bare metal. Some of the guys' boards are hand-made. Some of the checkers, too — rough-cut wood painted black and red. Other store-bought plastic checkers are chipped and scratched and dented from being slammed for emphasis in the fast-paced version called pool checkers.

Dudley plays about every day in Checker Park beneath the rumble and roar of the East-West Expressway that took his childhood home. On this Sunday, he joined a group of regulars.

Otis Hawkins, 76, supplied the checkerboard and the damaged checkers. Nathaniel Williams, 70, came directly from church, still dressed in his black suit, white shirt and tie. Chris Bradley, at 48 one of the young fellas, wore a plain white ball cap and matching T-shirt. He started playing when he was about 20 years old, already something of an anachronism in a generation that has drifted away from the challenge, strategy, intellect and one-upmanship of competitive checkers.

Playing checkers, he said, is how you stay out of trouble, escape your life, and meet the men who become your mentors.

"It occupies your time, your head, everything," he said. "You just forget all your problems when you're playing. And when you're done playing, you go right back to your problems."

The old men speak with reverence of Freeman Coney III, a Jones High School educator known to all as "Schoolboy."

Schoolboy was legendary, good enough in his day to compete in the 1969 American Pool Checkers Association national tournament in Atlanta, where he placed 13th out of 200 competitors. Schoolboy never taught Dudley how to play, but he taught him plenty of lessons. Three moves into the game, Schoolboy would declare victory.

"He would tell me how he was going to beat me before he beat me," Dudley said.

Schoolboy played pool checkers — where pieces can move back and forth and kings have free range — like an NBA point guard. He would move his checker while looking away or pretend to be distracted until his opponent made the wrong move.

Conley died in 2013 at age 81. He had a protégé, a man now in ill health who leaves the game to Dudley and the regulars.

On this day, a small group of men crowded quietly around Dudley as he played Williams. Nobody talked trash to the two men playing checkers. The players themselves said little. They used the loud slap of their checker against the board do all the talking: smack, smack, smack. A triple jump. Take that.

The time to talk is when the game ends with laughter and mock indignation by the losing player. The vanquished stands up and another player slides in to take his place, keeping the game going and the tradition alive for another game, another day.

March 10, 2014

Barrier Breakers: Orlando's First Black Police

The black-and-white photograph, taken in 1956, shows six police officers, guns in holsters, hands clasped behind their backs. It captures a seminal moment in the history of Orlando: the first black men to wear the uniform of the Orlando Police Department.

None grew up aspiring to become a policeman. In their youths, that was an impossibility. They were waiters, taxi drivers and cooks who broke the color barrier in law enforcement.

Some went on to long careers with the department. Others would move on to other cities, other jobs. Until now, little was written or known about these men. There is no mention of them in OPD's Hall of Fame.

They were all, by virtue of being the first, role models. And they were all, by virtue of being human, men with flaws.

Beginning today and for the next six days, the Orlando Sentinel will profile the men in the picture who made history.

***

A little after noon on a hot summer day in 1956, John W. Jordan parks his light-gray 1939 LaSalle at Mitchell's Service Station on the corner of Church and Terry streets.

Jordan is a tall, lean man in an Orlando policeman's uniform: brown shirt, tan slacks with a brown stripe. He carries a nickel-plated .38-caliber Smith & Wesson on his left hip. He substitutes the clip-on tie other officers wear for a necktie he can knot himself. He wears a Barney Fife-style cap with a badge above the brim. Another badge is pinned above his left breast pocket.

He walks east on Church Street, past the Chauffeurs, Bellmen, and Waiters Club where he spent some time while working at Morrison's cafeteria in downtown Orlando -- carrying the trays of white customers and busing away the dirty dishes. At a free-standing, two-story building of painted brick and Venetian blinds, he opens the front door to the Orlando Negro Chamber of Commerce. Five other black men join him -- all dressed in the same Orlando police uniforms. Z.L. Riley, who owns the men's-clothing store next door, is there, and so is E.B. Mitchell, whose photography studio is in the back of his house on Division Street.

Mitchell directs the men to the back of the chamber office and lines them up in front of a blank wall. Jordan had done this before, in 1952, when there were four black officers on the force.

He takes his place, second from the left. Mitchell asks the men to turn to their left and clasp their hands behind their backs. He tells them to move a little closer so that each man is lightly touching the body of the man on either side of him.

In the strict days of segregation, blacks are squeezed into a few square miles west of the railroad tracks. The six black officers patrol a few blocks of the black community's business district.

They joined the force as Orlando became one of the last major cities in Florida to integrate the Police Department, serving in an era when the Ku Klux Klan was active and the civil-rights movement was in its infancy.

Jordan -- the only one of the six still living -- leaves OPD in two years for Detroit. There, he will pursue a career as a songwriter and later marry the mother of Diana Ross. A man of many talents and big ambitions, Jordan is nicknamed "Gimmick" by a fellow officer. He left the Police Department under circumstances he still doesn't want to talk about.

On Jordan's right stands Richard Arthur Jones, who will become the first black man to make sergeant and lieutenant at OPD. Jones is 6-feet-2, 220 pounds. He was the first to apply to the Police Department and -- after waiting more than a year -- the first to be hired. His funeral 42 years later will be a belated tribute to his groundbreaking career.

On Jordan's left is Gainus Wright Jr., the youngest of the group at 23 and the only one with a college degree. Wright grew up in Orlando and played quarterback at Jones High School, where the girls adored him and teammates called him "Little Rock Wright." He will die before he can reach 50.

Next to Wright stands Mayo Howard, who will leave OPD the next year to become the first black man to wear the uniform of the Deerfield Beach Police Department. Thirty years later, after a distinguished career in Deerfield Beach, Howard's death, after a heart attack, will create a racial controversy in the town.

Beside Howard, his eyelids at half-staff, his gun sporting white handles, is Belvin Perry Sr., who would earn his reputation as a tough, no-nonsense street cop. The second black police officer hired by OPD, Perry will keep his job as a waiter after joining the force to help finance the college education of his children. Perry lives to see his five children become a judge, a lawyer, a surgeon, an educator and a business owner.

On the far right, with a Clark Gable mustache and a white-handled gun to match Perry's, is Otha Lee Kelly. Kelly will spend much of his time with OPD in the juvenile division, where he nurtures legions of safety crossing guards, some of whom will follow him into law enforcement.

"I look at those guys as the foundation for us black officers. It got started with them stepping to the plate to make it better for us as we came along," says Orlando City Commissioner Sam Ings, who joined the Orlando Police Department in 1973.

The picture took only seconds to snap. It was still midday, hours before the men would begin their night shift breaking up fights, arresting drunks, cracking down on illegal gambling and checking stores for burglaries. They left the building, walked down Church Street to their cars, drove home and changed clothes.

Jones went home to his first wife, Perry Lee, and his two

children in the same house on Jaxso Place where they lived when he was first hired by OPD. His hiring, and that of Perry, in 1951 was a landmark day in the black community. It went largely unnoticed in the white community.

Orlando in 1951 is a place of 52,000 people -- about 25 percent of them black and concentrated in less than 7 percent of the city's area.

The city has an Air Force base and the political commerce of a county seat, but Orlando is still largely an agricultural town with citrus groves radiating in all directions. The city's politics are of their day: Southern, white, conservative. Racial progress, when it comes, arrives slowly. In 1950, Orlando is the last city in Florida to allow blacks to vote in Democratic primaries.

Segregation is the law of the land and, in Orlando, strictly enforced. The black community in Orlando is concentrated in an area bordered by Orange Blossom Trail and Division, Amelia and Carter streets. Blacks can cross Division Street and the railroad tracks to work and shop in the white-owned businesses, but if two or more black men strayed across the line for reasons other than to make or spend money, there is a white police officer to intercept them.

"One going by himself was all right. If there was a group, they were not permitted," says Wolf Kahn, 85, who worked in a store on Church Street where the tracks divided the races.

The Ku Klux Klan is active and obvious in Orange County and neighboring counties. In 1950, there are several Klan rallies in Orlando and cross-burnings in the city. At the same time, the Orange County NAACP is becoming one of the state's most active chapters.

The tension of the opposing forces of segregation and equal rights boils to the surface in 1951, the year Jones and Perry break the color line.

In February, a black janitor is beaten and shot in the leg for allegedly entering the girls' restroom in a white elementary school unescorted. A month later, in an apparent case of mistaken identity, his brother-in-law is beaten, flogged and shot to death -- the only reported lynching in the United States in 1951. In July, an apartment building is dynamited after the owner rented an apartment to a black family. In November, the Creamette Frozen Custard Stand on Orange Blossom Trail is bombed for refusing to serve blacks and whites at separate windows.

"It was a flash point that year," says Benjamin D. Brotemarkle, author of Crossing Division Street: An Oral History of the African-American Community in Orlando. "People don't think of Orlando as there being any racial violence, but 1951 was a particularly bad year."

Leading up to that year of history and violence, the hiring of the first black officers in Orlando is done quietly behind the scenes. Again, Orlando lags behind the rest of the state. Sanford has black officers. Daytona Beach does, too. Miami hired its first black policemen in 1944. Tampa soon followed. Jacksonville added its first black to the police force in 1950.

The agent of change is Z.L. Riley, the slight, balding tailor who helped found the Orlando Negro Chamber of Commerce in 1945 along with a waiter named Arthur "Pappy" Kennedy. Kennedy will later become the first black person elected to the Orlando City Council, in 1973.

The Negro chamber is the conduit between the black community and the white establishment in Orlando. The activists in the black community -- the ministers, lawyers and civil-rights leaders -- push the agenda, but the message is delivered to Mayor William Beardall and the City Council by Riley and the chamber. Beardall was first elected in 1940. He, too, is a man of his time, culture and constituencies. Racial progress, under Beardall, comes with some reluctance, much foot-dragging, but no outright opposition.

"Beardall was a real old Cracker, but he wanted what was best for Orlando," says Wally Sanderlin, who was elected to the City Council in 1954.

Beardall gives Riley the green light to find someone who might qualify as the first black police officer. It's Pappy Kennedy who approaches Jones, a man he knows well from their days waiting tables together at Dubsdread Country Club.

Jones grew up in Orlando; served in the Army; has a wife, family, and good employment record. He is well-liked in the community. Most of all, he has the physique and tough disposition that command respect.

On Oct. 31, 1949, Richard Arthur Jones applies to become the first black police officer in Orlando. He doesn't quit his day job waiting tables at the all-white Orlando Country Club. Jones' application languishes. In February 1950, Riley is calling the city's Civil Service Board, which oversees the hiring of all police and fire personnel, asking why Jones has not received his physical exam. Jones takes his physical at the end of the month.

The doctor, city physician J.P. Williamson, notes on his exam: "This man is of above the average intelligence for his race."

In June, Jones receives a letter from the city informing him he has failed the physical because of high blood pressure and an irregular heartbeat.

"I have no alternative but to advise you that the Civil Service Board cannot accept your application," says a letter sent to Jones on June 13, 1950.

The disqualification of Jones doesn't squelch the demand from the black community for representation on the force. Leonard Fletcher, the chief examiner of the Civil Service Board, is told to find another Negro to become an officer. The man he picks is Belvin Perry Sr.

Perry is a waiter at Morrison's cafeteria, working alongside John W. Jordan during the day, and operating a pool hall on Parramore at night. He is 29 years old and spent four years in the Army before coming home to Orlando. He likes guns.

One day, his customer is Leonard Fletcher. Fletcher asks Perry whether he would consider becoming a police officer. Perry is making $11 a week at Morrison's, plus nickel and dime tips. His starting pay as an officer will be $220 a month.

He says yes. The city has what it wants: two men to become the first black police officers.

Fletcher tells Perry: "Go tell Jones to reapply."

February 18, 2007

Barrier Breaker: Richard Arthur Jones

On his first day on the job in January 1951, Richard Arthur Jones reported to work at an old school building on Jackson Street and Orange Avenue that had been converted into Orlando's City Hall. The Orlando Police Department, and jail, were in the basement. The police chief and detectives were on the first floor. He was given a nightstick, a weighted-leather slapjack and handcuffs. No gun, no radio, no patrol car. Jones and partner Belvin Perry Sr. would walk their 11 p.m.-to-7 a.m. beat from Parramore to Division, Church to Carter.

On their beat, they would check doors of closed businesses and vacant stores, break up dice games in the alley, crack down on bookies and "numbers" men selling bolita tickets, stop fights in bars, arrest drunks or just send them home. There weren't many guns on the streets then, but just about every man carried a knife.

In the 1950s, in Northern and Southern cities, black officers were hired to crack down on crime in the black community. Inside those boundaries, they were policemen. Outside their beat, they had no authority. They could detain whites but not arrest them, and they were not allowed to testify against whites in court.

The sight of the first two black police officers in Orlando, walking side by side down Church and Parramore, caused a stir among black residents. Most of the people Jones passed knew him. They went to school with him at Jones High and sat next to him at Ebenezer United Methodist Church. They knew when he left to join the Army in 1943 and when he came home after he got out in 1946. They saw him working in the warehouse at the Orlando Air Base and waiting tables at Dubsdread and Orlando country clubs.

But seeing Jones, along with Perry, in a police officer's uniform was like seeing him for the first time.

"It was amazing to see them in a uniform," said Juanita Hailey Sanders, 75, a retired school-cafeteria manager who graduated from high school the year Jones and Perry began walking the beat. "We were so proud, we just wanted to touch it."

In Richard Arthur Jones, the city of Orlando picked for its first black police officer a meticulous man, rigid in his habits, regimented in his routine. He always sat in the same pew in church -- third row from the back on the right -- and arrived early enough to make sure nobody got there before him. Dinner was always at 6 p.m. Not 5:59, not 6:01.

He was married to Perry Lee, his first wife who was a teacher at the time, and had two young children at home, a son and a daughter. His daughter Vicki's job was to prepare his uniform to his precise specifications -- transferring the pins, badge and nameplate from the used uniform on the left side of the bed to the freshly laundered shirt with extra starch on the right. At least part of his personality came from an awareness that he was being judged every day by whites, said Michael Brooks, his grandson.

"He was well aware of the meaning of being the first black police officer, the first black sergeant, the first black lieutenant," said Brooks, 32. "You were carrying the weight of the race on your shoulders. People wouldn't say Richard Jones was late -- they would say black people are late."

By nature a private man, Jones never spoke about the prejudices he encountered from white officers, but his family and friends were aware of the racial pressures within the police force.

All six black police officers in that photograph taken in 1956 would be suspended, demoted or dismissed over allegations that they didn't measure up to Police Department standards, according to their personnel files. It was a common occurrence among the South's first black police officers, who were often fired under the vague charges of "conduct unbecoming an officer," said W. Marvin Dulaney, director of the College of Charleston's African American Studies Program.

"They were held to a higher standard. They basically couldn't get away with anything," said Dulaney, author of Black Police in America.

Jones was suspended once for "conduct unbecoming an officer" for 10 days in 1969, but two years later he would become OPD's first black lieutenant by impressing both police Chief Robert Chewning and Mayor Carl Langford. Jones caught Langford's attention after bawling out the mayor for driving over some fire hoses -- until realizing whom he was talking to.

"He said, `Oh, I guess you are the only person I would allow to run over three fire hoses and not put into jail,' " said Langford, 87. "He was polite, straightforward, but not a brown-noser."

Family members said Jones was as reticent with his words as he was meticulous in his dress. He was a direct, no-nonsense kind of man who had little use for small talk or long conversations. You could spend all day in a boat with him fishing, and you'd end up with more fish than conversation, said his son Billy Williams, 63.

In 1976, 25 years after Jones and Perry joined the force together, they retired within a day of each other. Jones spent his retirement years working as a security guard at Tinker Field and the Central Florida Fair. Free from working weekends, he became more involved in his church, serving as chairman of the deacon board, working as an usher, and teaching Sunday school. Twice a week, he delivered Meals on Wheels.

Before his death, Jones suffered from Parkinson's disease. His big, strong body shriveled to skin upon bone. He would die in a nursing home Sept. 9, 1998, at age 76. His funeral at Ebenezer United Methodist Church spilled outside the doors. His coffin was carried by white and black Orlando officers to a hearse escorted by motorcycle cops to a cemetery in Apopka. Traffic was stopped along the East-West Expressway for the body of Richard Arthur Jones.

Treated like a second-class citizen for much of his time on the force, Jones was honored like a dignitary in death, said his daughter Vicki Jones-Brooks: "It was like a pouring out of what can we do as this last tribute to show honor and respect."

February 19, 2007

Barrier Breaker: John W. Jordan

John W. Jordan drops the phonograph needle on the edge of the 45 and, through the pops and crackles, comes a Christmas song recorded 25 years ago. "Merry Christmas to You Santa" was going to be "Jay" Jordan's ticket to fame and fortune. Today, he should be a successful songwriter, not an 84-year-old security guard living with his fourth wife in Richmond Heights.

"I should be a rich man by now," says Jordan, the last survivor of the six black police officers who posed for a group picture in 1956. "The whole world should be singing it every Christmas."

Wife No. 3 was the mother of Motown superstar Diana Ross, whom Jordan married in the 1970s. He had hopes that Ross might record the song, but instead it's the voice of Gywn Wells, who was married to his cousin.

The third black police officer hired by the Orlando Police Department, Jordan was working at Morrison's Cafeteria in downtown Orlando when Leonard Fletcher, chief examiner of Orlando's Civil Service Board, recruited him into the Orlando police force. He joined OPD in 1952, the same year as Johnnie L. Williams, who would leave OPD in about a year.

Not everybody in the black community was happy to have black police officers patrolling the streets. To some residents, the police were oppressors, the enforcers of the white man's apartheid, and any black men who joined the police were traitors to their race, Jordan says. And there were those who simply didn't like getting arrested. The shins of John Jordan still bear the marks where he was kicked by drunken women resisting arrest, and the scar on his left forearm shows where a man stabbed him with a knife.

To be a black police officer in the 1950s was to live a double life -- one for the white establishment, the other for your black neighbors, Jordan says.

"It was like having a dual personality," he says.

Even while he worked as a cop, Jordan always had interests outside the police force. He opened a snack stand and performed in a quartet. He wrote music and dreamed of becoming a professional musician. For all his talents and ambitions, his best friend on the police force, Gainus Wright Jr., nicknamed Jordan "Gimmick."

"I'm always coming up with something," Jordan says.

In his life, he has worked on locomotives, designed and built houses, painted pictures, worked as a security guard and owned a janitorial business. For a time, he studied graphic art so he could design album covers for Motown. That didn't work out.

Jordan was a strict father who insisted his three daughters speak with proper diction, keep the house immaculate and make sure their clothes were clean and ironed, said his oldest daughter, Vivian Carrington. Carrington said Jordan would buy her picture puzzles and time her on how fast it took her to put the pieces together. As a child, having a father who was one of the first black police officers was like living with a celebrity, she said.

"A lot of kids' parents had demeaning jobs. Our dad,

because he was a cop, it was like he was a movie star," Carrington said.

But by 1958, Jordan's career in law enforcement was over. He was dismissed from the force Oct. 9 for "conduct unbecoming an officer," according to his personnel file.

Jordan said he was working for a white woman who had a catering service. The woman was also a seamstress who made a wedding dress for Jordan's oldest daughter. He was at the woman's house, discussing the wedding, when two white OPD officers -- co-workers of his -- knocked on the woman's door. They told her they had a report of a burglary at her house and asked whether they could look around. In the kitchen, they found John Jordan sitting at the table. They took him back to the police station, locked him in a cell and told him that he would need to talk to the police chief the next day, Jordan says.

Fired from the Orlando Police Department, Jordan left for Detroit.

Jordan denies he was fired. He says he was suspended for three days without pay and resigned from the force in November 1958. The hurt from that time of his life still stings, and Jordan would not comment further for this story or have his picture taken.

In Detroit, Jordan would try unsuccessfully to join the Police Department and launch a music career. He would marry a second time, divorce, and then wed Ernestine Ross, who died in 1984. Thirty years after he left, Jordan moved back to Orlando in 1988. He didn't recognize the place -- and few remembered him.

"I feel like I've been forgotten," he says.

His face is broader than it was when he posed for that photograph of the six black police officers in 1956. His voice is raspy.

But his handshake is strong, his back is straight. He hasn't stopped working. And he hasn't stopped hoping that someday "Merry Christmas to You Santa" will be the next classic Christmas song.

"It will sell. People will buy this record, and the artists will record it," he says. "It will be just as popular as `White Christmas'."

February 20, 2007

Barrier Breaker: Gainus Wright Jr.

On his application to become an Orlando policeman in 1954, Gainus Wright Jr. included a picture of himself wearing his military-police helmet. In neat, printed handwriting, he wrote, "I'm making application because of my previous Army experience, because Orlando is a growing city and is greatly in need of police protection."

He was 23 years old, just two months out of the Army, and full of confidence. He had a college degree from Bethune-Cookman College in physical education. At Jones High School, he was a star athlete in basketball, baseball and football -- a quarterback so tough and competitive his teammates nicknamed him "Little Rock Wright."

"He liked to party and have fun. The girls loved him. I could never understand why girls would like him," said his younger sister Pinkie Sanders, 73.

Wright's father, Gainus Wright Sr., was chauffeur, gardener and right-hand man to one of the richest, most influential white men in Orlando: Dr. Philip Phillips. His mother, Letha J. Wright, owned a beauty shop on Parramore Avenue that Orlando's black police officers passed every day on their beat. He listed as one of his references John W. Jordan, the third black officer hired by OPD.

Wright had everything going for him and appeared on the fast track among the black police officers. In July 1959, Gainus Wright was promoted to probationary sergeant along with Richard Arthur Jones, who had become the department's first black officer in 1951. And then everything came crashing down.

A month after his promotion, Wright was demoted to patrolman for "conduct unbecoming an officer" on allegations of sleeping on the job. A white officer said he was driving down Church Street when he saw Gainus Wright Jr. sitting on a bench, his head down, asleep on duty. To his friends and family, the demotion was seen as another case of a black man who was viewed by his white co-workers as being too smart for his own good.

"If you're a black man living in a white man's world, you can be bright -- and be too smart," said Alzo Reddick, a former legislator who grew up on the streets patrolled by the black police officers.

Wright's father took his son's demotion to his employer, who helped the family hire a lawyer. In November 1959, the city's Civil Service Board overturned Wright's demotion, restored him to sergeant status and ordered the Police Department to award back pay. It was a short-lived triumph. Six months later, Gainus Wright Jr. would be demoted again for misconduct and resign from the police force.

"He felt there were people who didn't want them there. That is one of the reasons he left," Sanders said.

Wright's wife, a teacher, never really liked her husband's career choice.

"To be honest, I didn't think it was a job for a college graduate at the time. He could have been doing something else," said Lillian Thompson Wright, 75, who married Gainus in 1956.

With Lillian's encouragement, the couple moved to South Florida, where Wright became an elementary-school teacher. In his 14 years with Broward County schools, Wright would spend most of his time working with potential dropouts in middle school.

Once an athlete, Gainus Wright Jr. was always a smoker. Nothing his wife did could make him stop. In the last years of his life, suffering from emphysema, Wright breathed through a tube in his nose from a tank of oxygen.

Lillian was in the kitchen one day in January 1978 when she heard her husband gasping for breath in the bedroom.

"He started coughing, and it was hard for him to get a breath," his wife said. "I called the ambulance, and they took him to the hospital. He died that day."

Three days after his 47th birthday, Gainus Wright Jr. was dead.

Lillian Wright had her husband cremated. Half of his ashes went to his mother, who buried them beside his father in Washington Park Cemetery. The other half rest on the table beside Lillian's bed.

February 21, 2007

Barrier Breaker: Mayo Howard

When Evelyn first met Mayo Howard in 1951, she didn't think he was her type. Oh, he was handsome. He was charming. And -- the real attraction -- he could cook and sew.

But his skin was just too light.

"I'm a brown woman. And he was very light-skinned. During that period, people would stare," said Evelyn Howard, 74. "It was like black and white."

Mayo Howard was not so light-complexioned as to pass for white, but the Cherokee blood in his family and the shape and color of his hazel eyes gave Howard enough of a different look that many people were not sure of his racial identity.

"You could tell he's ethnic. You just didn't know what color he was," Evelyn Howard said.

When he died in 1985, the color of Mayo Howard's skin would cause an uproar in Deerfield Beach, where Howard became one of the first blacks on the police force after leaving the Orlando Police Department in 1957.

In Deerfield Beach, Mayo Howard achieved the success, acclaim and kudos that had eluded him in Orlando.

Howard was born in Tallahassee, the second of five children whose father was a machinist, said his sister Bertha Dupont. He graduated from high school and was playing football at Florida A&M his freshman year when he broke his leg and dropped out of college, Dupont said. After leaving school, he served in the Army before moving to Orlando.

Howard was working as a cook at Morrison's Cafeteria, where he was good friends with Belvin Perry Sr., when he joined the Police Department in 1954. He was 29 at the time, married to his first wife, Clyde Mae, and had five young children at home. As a police officer he would make $260 a month.

A serious man, Howard had a way of dealing with people that made him a good officer, said Charlie Jean Salter, his first wife's sister.

"He could relate to anyone. No matter what status you had in life, he could relate to you," Salter said.

His son Maurice E. Howard said joining the Police Department was a dream come true for Mayo Howard: "I know my dad always wanted to be a cop."

That dream ended for Howard in Orlando when he was dismissed from the force on allegations of "misconduct of an officer." His last day was Nov. 7, 1957. A few months later, Deerfield Beach police hired Howard to patrol the city's black neighborhoods. Two other black men preceded Howard on the force, but he was the first to wear the same uniform as white officers and the first to arrest whites as well as blacks, said Deerfield Beach Commissioner Sylvia Portier.

"Although he was hired for the black community, he didn't adhere to that. He would arrest you if you were white, yellow or brown. That's what you liked about Mayo Howard," Portier said.

Rising to the rank of lieutenant, Howard started the Police Department's school-liaison program, worked with kids interested in law enforcement through the Explorers club, and helped create a center for teens, his wife said.

He earned the respect of both the white and black

communities.

"He was a kindhearted person who was respected all around," said Beulah Hill, 58, who helped get a park in her neighborhood named for Mayo Howard in 1997. "He wasn't just a policeman. He was more of a social worker. If we had a problem, we went to Mr. Howard."

At Mayo Howard's house, white and black were equally welcome. The dining-room table might find the city's white mayor or a black congressman, said his son Delano Howard. Color didn't matter to Mayo.

Delano remembers, back when he was 10 or 11 years old, Mayo Howard bringing home a severely sunburned Scandinavian tourist who had his clothes and money stolen after falling asleep on the beach. Nobody else had offered to help the man.

"My dad is dragging him to a black neighborhood, looking like a lobster. He stayed for two weeks," said Delano Howard, 39. "It really touched me that this is how you are supposed to be in life. This is what makes you human."

In 1985, a few days before Christmas, Mayo Howard had a heart attack while still working as a police officer. In the hospital, Howard fell, hit his head and died. He was 60 years old.

Evelyn Howard said the Deerfield Beach police chief told her not to worry about Howard's funeral -- the department would handle everything. Plans were made to bury him in the city-owned Deerfield Beach Memorial Cemetery next to two other distinguished Deerfield Beach police officers.

"The chief made all the arrangements. I didn't have anything to do with his funeral arrangements, except to pick out the casket. They decided where he was to be buried, not me," Evelyn said.

The police chief didn't know that the cemetery, under deed restrictions going back to 1933, was for whites only.

Denied burial beside the white officers in Memorial Cemetery, Mayo Howard was laid to rest in Pineview Cemetery

-- the city's black graveyard. Insulted and humiliated, Evelyn Howard sued Deerfield Beach to have her husband exhumed and reburied at Memorial Cemetery.

"My husband served Deerfield. He didn't just work for one segment of the city, he worked for the entire city," Evelyn said.

The lawsuit alienated the Howards from the Police Department Mayo Howard had served for 27 years and the black community he had lived with since 1958.

"The city I grew up in, they just turned on us," Delano said. "I had people say, `Is your dad too good to be buried in the black cemetery?' "

Two years later, the Deerfield Beach City Council settled the lawsuit out of court -- agreeing to allow Mayo Howard to be buried in Deerfield Beach Memorial Cemetery.

His gravestone is a bronze marker with raised letters that identify him as a staff sergeant in the Army. One of the first blacks hired by the Orlando Police Department, Mayo Howard, in death, became the first black buried in a cemetery of 1,500 whites.

February 22, 2007

Barrier Breakers: Belvin Perry Sr.

It was a windy day in 1993, too windy to fish, so Belvin Perry Sr. stayed home and polished his guns inside the house on Domino Drive that he built on a waiter's tips and a policeman's salary.

A man who never finished high school, Perry emphasized education to his children, who grew up to become a school principal, a business owner, a surgeon, a lawyer and a judge.

His son, the judge, came to visit that morning. Belvin Perry Jr. was sitting on the bed in the guest room as his father wiped down his rifles and put them back into the Fort Knox safe in the corner of the room. Retired from the Orlando Police Department for 17 years, Belvin Perry Sr. loved guns. He loved hunting. He shot quail, dove and deer. And the occasional bad guy.

In his 25 years with OPD, Belvin Perry Sr. was known as a tough street cop who could defuse a tense situation with his tongue -- or a bullet from his gun. In 1957, Perry was found justified in shooting a man three times after he wrestled away Perry's nightstick and then came at him with a knife. Through the years, the story enlarged into legend, reinforcing the image of Belvin Perry as a cop who didn't take lip from anybody.

"Perry had the reputation of being a no-nonsense kind of police officer. He was a cop's cop," said Jerry Demings, Orlando's first black police chief.

If Perry caught you breaking the law, you didn't expect him to cut you any slack, said John W. Jordan, his partner in the 1950s: "He was strict with the law. If he gave you a chance, you'd better take it and go. There wasn't any second time around."

But that street-cop toughness was tempered with a compassion for the people whose oath he took to serve and protect. Belvin Perry Jr. remembers his father promising a man who had no family that he would have a decent burial when he died. Perry Sr. pulled his children out of school that day to attend the man's funeral. At the grave site, there was no one there except the Perry family.

Of the six black police officers in the picture taken in 1956, Belvin Perry Sr. is the smallest, at 5 feet, 9 inches and about 160 pounds. But he knew everybody in town and how to talk most of them into doing what he wanted.

"My dad had a way with words. He knew how to talk to people, and he knew how to take care of himself even though he was slightly built," said Belvin Perry Jr., chief judge of the circuit court.

Perry Sr. grew up in Sanford as the only child of a single mother. He attended Crooms Academy but never made it past

10th grade, leaving school to work in the celery fields. It would be the one great regret of his life -- failing to finish high school -- and he was determined that his children would go to college. He continued working as a waiter at Morrison's Cafeteria even after joining the Police Department in 1951. He would wait tables and bus dishes during the day, go home, sleep, and get up at 6 p.m. to work the late shift at the Police Department from 11 p.m. to 7 a.m.

On his off-duty hours, Perry took whatever job he could find -- security work or waiter duty at holiday parties -- to pay for his children's education. He sent four children to college. One became a teacher, one a surgeon, one a lawyer and one a judge. Another son become a business owner.

As a father, Perry was as strict at home as he was tough on the street. If he didn't like the way the lawn was mowed or the garage was cleaned, it had to be done again. One time, when Perry Jr. was home for the summer from Tuskegee College, he spilled beer in the car he had borrowed from his father to go to work.

"Young man, how old are you?" his father said.

"You know how old I am," the son replied.

"You're 18 years old. You're not supposed to be drinking," Perry Sr. said. "If I hear you've been drinking beer, I'm going to arrest you and put you in jail myself."

His father didn't take him to jail, but he did take away the car keys. For the next month, Perry Jr. walked or took the bus to his summer job cleaning floors at a hospital.

Perry and Richard Arthur Jones both joined the police force at the same time and retired the same time. But while Jones would rise to the rank of lieutenant, Perry remained a patrolman all his life. He took the sergeant's test three times and never won a promotion. After a while, he stopped taking the test for advancement and resigned himself to a career as a beat cop.

Then in 1974, Perry was suspended for 28 days for "conduct unbecoming an officer" -- a common refrain for all six officers in the photo at a time when black officers were under extra scrutiny. Before he was transferred back to the night shift, Belvin Perry Sr. decided to retire, said his wife, Jessie.

After leaving the department in April 1976, Perry worked as a bellhop at Howard Johnson and looked after the rental property he owned. He served as deacon at Shiloh Baptist Church, volunteered at the senior center and delivered Meals on Wheels to the elderly. His passion remained fishing and hunting.

On that windy day in 1993, as his father polished his rifles, Belvin Perry Jr. was telling his dad about taking his own son on a tour of college campuses. The son followed the father into the family room, where Belvin Perry Sr. sat down in his favorite recliner.

But when he tried to talk to his son, no words came out. His lips were twisted, contorted. Belvin Perry Sr. was having a stroke. He would never speak again.

In the final years, before his death in 1995 at age 74, Belvin Perry Sr. lived at Conway Lakes Nursing Home. Once a week, there was a reunion in his room of the first three black police officers in Orlando. John W. Jordan would drive by the house of Richard Arthur Jones, who was suffering from Parkinson's disease, and they would visit Perry in the nursing home. Jones and Jordan would reminisce, Perry would listen, and before the visit was over, all three would fall asleep in their chairs.

February 23, 2007

Barrier Breakers: Otha Lee Kelly

In Otha Lee Kelly's house, the rules were strict, the consequences swift. Bad grades and you couldn't ride your bike for six weeks. Get a D on your report card, and you were out of the school band.

As one of the most visible black police officers in Orlando -- the man who introduced schoolchildren to law enforcement, who mentored school crossing guards, who chased down truants, who appeared on TV and wrote a newspaper column -- Kelly held his five children to a high standard in the 1950s and '60s. He expected their behavior to reflect his stature. And as a teenager approaching 20, Roger Kelly chafed under his father's restrictions. After a scolding from his dad for staying out too late, Roger Kelly told him that if it was his way or the highway, he would hit the road.

"Come with me," Otha Kelly told his son, and they drove to Sterchi's Furniture Store on Orange Avenue. There, the father bought his son a couch and a chair.

"Tell me where you want it delivered," Otha Kelly said.

"I moved out for a while," said Roger Kelly, now a 48-year-old minister. "But then I realized that staying out wasn't that important to me. I came back home and finished college."

Otha Lee Kelly was a 29-year-old cab driver when he was recruited by Belvin Perry Sr., the second black man hired by the Orlando Police Department, to become an officer in 1954. The pay for a black police officer was $245 a month. His wife, Alice, was aghast at his decision to take such a hazardous job.

"I did not like what I heard. I thought it would be too dangerous," said Alice Kelly, 75. "He said he needed to make more money and do something else. I was sad about it for a while, but I knew he was determined."

Kelly's talent as a police officer was his outgoing personality. He knew how to relate to people -- how to make them feel at ease with his sense of humor and the wisdom of his logic. It made him an ideal candidate when the department created a youth division and needed a police officer in Orlando's black schools.

"He was one of my best juvenile officers. The kids would really open up to him," said Don Van Scoyoc, 77, a white officer who worked with Kelly.

In the 1960s, Officer Kelly was the first black police officer that a generation of schoolchildren would see. He enticed them to join the safety patrol and then accompanied the children on annual field trips to Washington. Some would go on to become police officers themselves.

The first time Kenneth Walker saw Otha Kelly, he was 7 years old at Holden Street Elementary. Kelly came in with his black-and-white, reel-to-reel movies of Jiminy Cricket talking about bicycle safety and the importance of looking both ways before crossing the street. Later, Walker would enlist as a safety-patrol crossing guard under Kelly's tutelage so that when he reached sixth grade, he could march through the streets of Washington with thousands of other elementary-school crossing guards.

Kelly had a deep, resonant voice that sounded to Walker like the voice of God when admonishing a safety-patrol student on the correct way to do things.

"Officer Kelly took safety patrol personally. It was about integrity, honesty, dependability," said Walker, a captain with the Orange County Sheriff's Office.

Kelly was promoted to sergeant in 1962 and became a sergeant in the juvenile division a year later. But in 1975, Kelly was demoted to patrolman on allegations of "conduct unbecoming an officer," which he denied. After 21 years on the police force, he was back to where he had started in 1954. A year later, along with Perry and Richard Arthur Jones -- the first two black officers hired -- he retired after 22 years on the force.

Three months after he left OPD, Otha Kelly applied to become a "permanent substitute" teacher at Carver Middle School. At the same time, he managed an investment group he started with a brother and some friends that bought rental property and businesses in Orlando and Brevard County. He taught school for several years and managed the apartments until his death from cancer, five days after his 62nd birthday, in 1986.

"He died when I was 16," said Raymer Kelly, 36, his youngest child. "I felt sort of cheated. My other brothers and sister had a lot longer time with him."

Kelly found a videotape of his father speaking to a sixth-grade class in 1972. When he hears his dad's voice, so strong and resolute, it turns him back into the boy who wanted only to measure up to his father's expectations.

When he sees the pictures, he feels the pride of a son whose father set an example for those who followed. It's the same feeling that comes to the spouses and children of all six of those black men who posed for a picture inside the Orlando Negro Chamber of Commerce on a sunny, bright summer day in 1956.

"It's like I'm looking at history," Raymer Kelly said. "People in the black community, these were their heroes."

February 24, 2007

Life Inside Extended Stay Motels

The motel room rents by the week. A pair of generic pastel seaside paintings hangs on the walls. The carpet is worn and stained. A round table and two chairs are upholstered in seen-better-days green.

It's the kind of place along the tourism strip of U.S. Highway 192 in Kissimmee that attracts budget-conscious tourists who spend their big bucks on the theme parks down the road.

But families live here, too -- mothers and fathers with three or four children, couples with newborn babies.

They came to Orlando looking for decent jobs and good weather. But what they found were low wages and apartments they can't afford. Now they exist inside the 12-by-21-foot boxes, living here for months, sometimes years. For them, even owning a trailer is an unattainable dream.

This is a week in their lives at the Sun Florida Inn.

The Bronkeys

Ivan Bronkey stands in the drizzle, smoking a Marlboro while leaning against the door of his 1984 Ford Country Squire station wagon with the missing hood ornament. The rain on his face feels good, reminding him of home, back in Oregon.

"We call it cloud sweat," he says. "It's not rain until you can't see that car."

The family's odyssey from Portland to San Diego to Pensacola to Orlando in search of work wasn't meant to end up here, in a room the size of a self-storage unit. After two years at the Sun Florida Inn, a motel room can feel like a prison cell for a family of five.

"You get in here, and it's hard to get out," says Bronkey, 34, a bus driver by trade.

So they're stuck in a place they never intended to stay. Ivan allows no one inside their room. Their children -- 12-year-old Adriana, 9-year-old Minda, and 7-year-old Joey -- are seldom seen outdoors.

There are neighbors out there you don't want to know.

"It's hard on the kids," says Bronkey's wife, Karissa, who is home-schooling their children. "This is not a place where I want them to go outside. You don't know who's in the room next door to you. You don't know where they come from."

Like many girls her age, Minda yearns for her own room away from her annoying younger brother and bossy older sister.

"I've never had my own room. I need my own room," she pleads.

Minda's parents understand the stigma that comes from living in a motel.

"I'm very protective of who I tell," says Karissa, 31. "It's hard to make friends and tell them that after two years we're still in a motel. You want to make friends, but you can't invite them over. And because you can't invite them over, they won't invite you over either."

The extended-stay motel is the first stop for families who have packed everything they own into a car to find a better life in Orlando and the last refuge for low-wage workers who don't have the cash, credit or clean record to move into an apartment.

Folks like the Bronkeys move here expecting to stay a couple of weeks, until they can get a job and find an apartment. But in rooms that start at $165 a week, there is little left at the end of the week for those making $6.85 an hour cleaning motel rooms, $6.70 operating rides at Disney World or $30 a day digging construction footers.

Bronkey makes good money by extended-stay-motel standards -- $10.17 an hour -- working the night shift on a Disney crew that cleans 267 buses. The Bronkeys are one of the few families at the motel that owns two cars: the old station wagon and a 1992 GMC van that leaks water but gets Karissa to her massage-therapy classes.

Of the nearly dozen families with children in the 48-room motel, the Bronkeys would seem the most likely to leave, yet have been there the longest.

"When we got here, we had a lot of hope. He got his job pretty much right away. I thought I'd finish school and get a massage job pretty quickly. But the longer we're here, the less we can put away," Karissa says.

Sun Florida Inn residents have all done the math. They know they are spending as much as $840 a month to stay in the motel, but to get into an apartment would cost them from $1,600 to $1,800.

Lacking kitchens, many motel residents end up spending more on fast food than groceries. There's gas for the guzzler. A 90-minute bus ride to a job at Disney costs $1.25 each way. After that, and the weekly rent, what's left is often consumed by car repairs and doctor bills.

The chance of moving from motel to apartment further declines for those with poor credit or criminal records. The extended-stay motels are filled with flawed people who left behind their problems but can't escape their pasts.

Most everybody at the Sun Florida Inn has something missing or broken. Marriages. Cars. Teeth. Some lack education. Some have criminal records. Some have drug and alcohol problems. Some can't catch a break.

The Bronkeys say the blemish on their credit history is a roommate's eviction that they've been unable to expunge from their record.

The Thomases

In the summer, when the school bus stopped in front of the Sun Florida Inn, the only student who stepped on was 8-year-old Lashawn Thomas.

Now that school has started, there are sometimes 10 children waiting for the bus outside the Sun Florida Inn.

In June, Lashawn's mother, Valarie Thomas, received a notice from the Osceola schools that her kids were eligible for a reading program at Central Elementary. When she checked it out, she found the program was for homeless children.

"If you live in a motel, they consider you homeless. Homeless? I think homeless is when you are in the street," says Thomas, 33.

But to the school system, life in a motel is as transient and uncertain as living inside a car or out in the woods. Raising her children inside a motel room, Thomas is trying to teach them that dignity resides inside the self, not in a place.

"You can live in a motel and still speak properly and carry yourself properly," Thomas says.

But there is a shame that sticks like sweat to motel residents. Her husband, who makes $8.50 an hour as a security guard at an Orlando hotel, doesn't tell his co-workers where he lives. Valarie hedges when people ask, saying only that she lives at the Sun Florida Inn.

Inside their room, Thomas keeps the children on a strict schedule. TV off after lunch. Read or color until 5 p.m. TV and dinner till 6:30 p.m. Showers at 7 p.m. Bedtime at 8 p.m., asleep by 9 p.m.

With little money left over at the end of the week, the Thomas family's chief form of entertainment is wishful thinking. The Thomases take drives to look at the model homes at Poinciana, dreaming of the day they leave the motel for a house.

"The first thing when I go into a house, I look for the kitchen," she said. "I go for a big kitchen."

Cassandra and Luis

For many of Orlando's low-wage workers, the pay-by-the-week motels along 192 become the catch basin for broken dreams.

In Osceola County, where the median-family income of $42,000 lags $5,000 behind Orange County and nearly $15,000 below Seminole County, the families inside the motels struggle to make even half that amount.

For Cassandra Cervantes, her 21-year-old husband, Luis, and their newborn baby, life is hard. The couple moved to Orlando in 2002 from a small town in Missouri, where the only job Luis could find was as a handyman.

The better life Cassandra and Luis expected has been a mixed blessing. The work is here, but the pay is low. The baby was born, and Luis lost his construction job. They bought a car for $150, and a month later it broke down. They paid the repairman $350 to fix it, and then he wanted $425 more.

"With the way our luck's going, every time we are doing good, everything is fine, something happens. That's our luck," says Cassandra Cervantes, 22.

Luis has been arrested twice on charges of battery -- once after being accused of giving Cassandra a black eye. After his second arrest, they lost their apartment and moved into the Sun Florida Inn in October.

"Before he went to jail, we used to fight all the time. We just have arguments now," Cervantes says. "Sometimes we argue about money. Sometimes it's about me not having the room picked up, or dinner's not ready or it's not what he wants."

Before the baby, Cassandra worked as a motel housekeeper, cleaning 16 rooms in eight hours for $6.85 an hour. When she lost her ride, she lost her job. After that, she worked at Wal-Mart for $6.75 an hour. The most her husband has made pouring concrete is $150 a day. Many times it's $40 or less a day.

When Luis is between jobs, Cassandra has to beg relatives for money to pay the weekly rent. The last time it was her father in Missouri.

"He said, `This is it. Don't call me for another favor. Don't call me if the baby is out of formula or needs diapers. I'm not paying it,' " Cervantes says.

If they can get their car back, Cassandra can get a job as a waitress. She has never worked as a waitress, but Denise, who lives at the motel, says you can make up to $150 a night.

The man working on their car is another Sun Florida Inn resident, a friend doing them a favor. But the auto-repair shop is owned by the man's father, who says: No money, no car.

No money, no car. No car, no money. It's Tuesday. The rent is due Friday. Cassandra fears eviction. If they lose their motel room, they might lose their 5-day-old daughter, Alexandria.

But as they are eating cheese tacos cooked in an electric skillet, the phone rings. Somebody needs a man to work concrete and will pick Luis up the next morning at 8:30.

In the next three days, Luis loads and unloads 600 concrete blocks and pours concrete for a miniature-golf attraction on

International Drive. For a 12-hour day, he is paid $72-- $6 an hour. When it comes time for the rent, he is $15 short.

Cassandra wears her worry like the tattoos on her arm and ankle. She is a thin-faced woman with large glasses framing eyes that seem often on the verge of tears.

When Luis returns from talking to the motel manager, Cassandra is waiting for him in their room.

"Did they let you?" she asks.

"Till next week," he replies.

This week, it was something good. Next week, it might be something bad.

"I don't see us getting out of here any time soon," Cervantes says. "If we do, it will be a miracle."

The Hyllebergs

Madysen Rayne Hylleberg is the princess of the Sun Florida Inn, a blond, 4-year-old social butterfly on a Whiz Kids 2 bike with training wheels.

Madysen rides bikes with the motel manager's kids. She collects nickels and dimes from the neighbors who purchase Kool-Aid at her lemonade stand. Madysen is the fantasy girlfriend of every boy in the motel younger than 8.

Her dad, the motel's maintenance man, cleans the pool, blows the leaves, cuts the grass and tries to keep the place clean of the kind of people he doesn't want his daughter around. The bickering couple who took their drunken fights to the upstairs balcony -- out. The mother of four with a boyfriend who was dealing drugs -- out.

All part of the job.

"When you turn a motel into an apartment," says Kevin Hylleberg, 40, "you have to deal with people's bad habits."

Along with the families, the extended-stay motels along 192 attract drug addicts, prostitutes, thieves and fugitives.

"There is some drug activity. There are prostitutes that are out there," Osceola County sheriff's Deputy Sharise Swan says. "For all you know, there could be a sexual predator from out of state staying there for a while. I would absolutely not allow my child to run around."

The Hyllebergs, like other Sun Florida Inn families, have filled their little room with all they own -- clothes, books, computers, baby strollers, TV sets, frying pans, toys. Hylleberg and his wife, Denise, have tried to make the motel room feel like a home. They've rearranged the furniture to create imaginary rooms -- a kitchen, a den, two bedrooms.

Others refuse to add anything of themselves to their rooms, fearing that making them more comfortable will make them harder to escape.

Hylleberg, his 34-year-old waitress wife, and Madysen moved into the Sun Florida Inn three months ago. Hylleberg says they expect to be here a year, save a little money, then move on to something better.

"It's just a pit stop," Hylleberg says.

In a place where everyone expects to leave in a couple of weeks, maybe a month, the average stay at the Sun Florida Inn lasts three months. After that, cabin fever starts to set in, Hylleberg says.

Hylleberg, who left Wisconsin after 14 years as a foundry worker, thinks of the Sun Florida Inn as a working vacation on the way to the Florida Keys -- a place he once visited as a boy.

"All I remember is it was gorgeous. I don't know what is there now, but we're going to find out," he says.

In the play-it-by-ear lifestyle common to so many extended-stay residents, Hylleberg doesn't know what he'll do for a living in the Keys and doesn't care. They're just chasing the dream.

"Ain't no rule says you have to stay in the same place your whole life," he says. "We'll decide when we get there."

Maggie and Angel

They arrived from New York on a Greyhound bus with $1,500 and Maggie eight months pregnant. After a month at the Sun Florida Inn, the money is gone, the last of it stolen with Angel's wallet.

"We thought we'd have a place to live, he'd get a job in a week," says Maggie, 31. "Then he lost his job and things started to fall apart."

They don't give their last names. Nobody gives last names in New York City, Angel says.

After they arrived, Angel, 22, worked three weeks at a resort, delivering towels and linens to maids until they found out he didn't have a drivers license. Now he has no job, no money and a baby boy.

To survive this week, Angel is trying to pawn his stack of Yu-Gi-Oh! game trading cards. It's an $800 deck, he says. One card is worth $160, maybe.

"My deck is unbeatable," he boasts.

In New York, he easily could get $200 from a pawnshop. But in Kissimmee, he can't find any pawnshop that takes decks of trading cards. It's Tuesday. The rent is due Friday.

"This week's rent? Who knows. Hopefully, I'll get rid of these cards," Angel says.

Maggie has another plan. Her mother is coming Thursday to see Gabriel, her first grandchild. When Mom's here, she'll take them to look for apartments. When Mom's here, they're going to Disney World. When Mom's here, there will be food in the refrigerator and the rent paid.

On the day of her mother's arrival, Maggie dresses Gabriel in a white and powder-blue outfit with booties and mittens and a knit cap over his bald, 4-week-old head. Gertrude Parucker didn't discourage her daughter's move to Orlando. Maggie and Angel were living in a dumpy hotel in Rockaway Beach. Maggie was pregnant. Angel couldn't find a job. Orlando looked good.

"If you want to work in this country, there are plenty of jobs -- especially in Florida, which is booming in tourists," says Parucker, 61, who drives a school bus in New Jersey and works for a caterer in the summer.

But this is not what Gertrude Parucker wants for her daughter -- living in a motel room, broke and unemployed. Maggie went to college, she worked in accounting, she had an apartment. And now she's living in a messy motel room where neighbors walk in and help themselves to food and cigarettes without asking.

"I couldn't live like this," Parucker says. "I want better for

Maggie."

Parucker helps her daughter organize the motel room. She buys her shelving, food, a microwave, a bottle sterilizer, a breast pump, a baby stroller and a car seat, which Maggie and Angel can use if they ever get a car. She takes them to Disney World, although the heat and the lines cut the day short before the fireworks explode over Cinderella Castle.

Along with the money she spends comes free advice: Get a plan; use some common sense; put a lock on your refrigerator to discourage the moochers; tell your boyfriend to get a job; find work yourself; stop lusting for things you can't afford; start watching your money.

When Maggie casually mentions her desire for a pedicure, her mother's retort is like a gunshot: "Pedicure! You need to pay your rent first. You live in La-La Land."

Before she leaves, Parucker pays the week's rent -- as much for her new grandson as her only daughter: "They take your child away if you don't have a roof over your head."

Angel, who hopes to catch on with Disney, still expects better days ahead. They can make it out of here, he says. Others have.

"If she gets a job and I get a job, we'll definitely have an apartment in a month or two," he says.

But in her four days at the Sun Florida Inn, Gertrude Parucker sensed something insidious, almost druglike, about the place.

"Some people, it becomes a habit," she says. "They stay there too long."

The Bronkeys' New Dream

The Bronkeys and their three children have spent two years trying to escape the Sun Florida Inn, but they haven't given up on their dream: owning a place of their own.

On this Tuesday, Ivan Bronkey pours a quart of oil into the engine of the old Ford station wagon, piles his family inside and points the land yacht toward St. Cloud.

Along the way, Ivan and Karissa talk about the places they have lived before their life was reduced to a single motel room. There was the two-story town-house apartment in Portland with the balcony that overlooked the city. There was the place in San Diego with the gas barbecue, pool and hot tub.

"It seems like a long time ago," Karissa says. "It seems like another life sometimes."

They meet the real-estate agent at the gated entrance to Shelter Cove, a mobile-home park on the shores of Lake Center with a bathhouse, community pool and a clubhouse shaped like a steamboat. They follow Realtor Emily Berry -- "The Queen of Shelter Cove" -- to a trailer with a wooden picnic table and an orange tree outside.

The one-bedroom trailer, with the lot, is listed for $18,500. At 224 square feet, it is 28 square feet smaller than their Sun Florida Inn motel room. But inside the trailer, there's a separate bedroom with a door, etched-glass cabinets, a refrigerator, a sofa that converts into a bed, and a kitchen table that turns into another bed.

Adriana stakes claim to the sofa wedged into the trailer's pop-out alcove.

"You know what I was thinking?" she tells her mother. "If I get the couch, we could put some draperies up and it could be sort of my own room."

Minda, who put the dibs on the kitchen table/bed, likes what she sees.

"I can imagine myself living here," she says.

Joey is ready to sign the offer sheet.

"Mom," he says, "we want this to be our new home."

This is no dream home for the Bronkeys, but it's not a motel room either. The trailer is small but significant.

The Bronkeys want a life that is not paid for in weekly installments. They want a place that is a home, not a room. They want to feel normal again.

The dream of a better life they arrived with two years ago has been squeezed down, condensed like a trash compactor, into the simple desire of escaping from an extended-stay motel.

"This is not normal. This is not right. My wife knows it. My kids know it," Ivan says. "The dream is to get out of here."

EPILOGUE

Here is what has happened to the residents at the Sun Florida Inn since the week in July that the Sentinel spent documenting their lives.

The Thomases: Valarie Thomas' children are back in school, and the family still lives at the Sun Florida Inn.

Cassandra and Luis: Cassandra Cervantes is working as a motel housekeeper, and her husband, Luis, is still working construction. They still live at the Sun Florida Inn.

The Hyllebergs: Kevin, Denise and Madysen Hylleberg moved to another motel last week.

Maggie and Angel: Maggie got a job as a waitress, and Angel is working in telephone sales. They still live at the Sun Florida Inn.

The Bronkeys: The Bronkeys did not get the mobile home. After two years at the Sun Florida Inn, they moved to another extended-stay motel on U.S. 192.

September 19, 2004

Faces in the Crowd: Illegal Immigration

The trailer park is a dump. Old tires lean against shacks. Toys and trash are strewn outside the trailers. Bare wood peeks through peeling paint like a face behind the blinds. A man inside a dumpster tosses empty cans to his buddy. Overhead, a helicopter hovers.

A blue Chevy sedan plows through the soft, sandy roads of the trailer park. The doors pop open and two men dressed in green uniforms jump out.

"You take the back; I have the front," says Border Patrol agent Marty Trevino.

Agent Wayne Baehre runs to the rear of trailer 65. He stands to one side, his hand on the revolver in his holster.

Trevino knocks on the door. Nobody answers. He knocks again.

There are people inside. A television is on.

Trevino says something in Spanish. Nobody opens the door.

The people inside, suspected illegal immigrants, know the rules. The Border Patrol has no search warrants. They can't come inside if you don't let them in.

While Baehre and Trevino try to coax the occupants outside, the trailer park is leaking illegals. As the agents move on, they find doors left open, trailers freshly vacated.

"We're burned here," Baehre says, and orders the Immigration and Naturalization Service helicopter to leave.

They end up arresting three young men, one riding in a pickup truck that tries to maneuver inconspicuously past the agents. The man inside catches the eye of Trevino, a Border Patrol agent for 13 years.

"When he saw us, his eyes got real wide and he looked straight ahead like, if he doesn't see me, I won't see him," says Trevino, 33, who was born in Chicago to Mexican parents.

The Border Patrol agents see what nobody else notices - a vast, invisible underground of illegal residents. Everywhere they look, they see people who come here to disappear into the multinational diversity of Central Florida.

Last year, they picked up illegals from 39 nations.

They arrest Mexicans cutting sod in Osceola County, chopping ferns in Volusia County, digging ditches in Seminole County, building offices in Orange County.

They find illegal immigrants from South Africa working as tennis pros in Seminole. Canadian flight instructors in Brevard. British pub owners in Kissimmee. French nannies in Maitland. Filipino nurses in Orlando. Guatemalan landscapers in Winter Park. Pakistani clerks, Haitian cooks, Honduran maids on International Drive.

They search for Chinese nationals who disappear from their jobs at Splendid China and Moroccans who walk away from their Epcot pavilion.

"This is a large melting pot of illegals from all over the world," says Baehre, 44, who grew up in Buffalo, N.Y., the son of a Polish mother and German father.

The number of illegals arrested by Orlando Border Patrol agents topped 1,300 in 1995 - the largest number since 1983. Of the 5,861 illegal immigrants they have arrested since 1990, 17 percent were deported for committing crimes in the United States.

An estimated 322,000 illegal immigrants - about 1 in 10 nationwide - live in Florida, which ranks behind California and New York. Most reside in South Florida, but Central Florida is a mecca of economic opportunity for illegal immigrants.

They swarm to jobs in construction, agriculture and tourism, where workers are in short supply and turnover is high. Some take jobs from Americans; others do work no American wants.

After September, their chances of escaping detection will improve when the U.S. Immigration and Naturalization Service plans to close the five-agent office that patrols Volusia, Brevard, Lake, Orange, Seminole and Osceola counties.

About 30 interior Border Patrol stations nationwide are being eliminated as the INS shifts resources toward stemming the flow of illegal immigrants from Mexico. The closings are part of a plan to add 5,000 new agents along the Rio Grande River - twice the number now stationed on the Mexican border.

"The gist of it is to get the Border Patrol back on the border," says Baehre, who drifted into the Border Patrol after trying carpentry, selling insurance and working in a center for mentally handicapped children.

Baehre's been to the border. He spent the first seven of his 18 years with the Border Patrol in Del Rio, Texas. He doesn't want to go back.

"The border is your initiation into the Border Patrol. It's your hell on earth," Baehre says.

It's Mexicans dashing across the line while agents are pelted by an artillery of rocks and bottles. It's people who shed layers of clothing like chameleons to change their appearances as they're being pursued.

It's Texas heat and border boredom, frustration and anger, and beneath it all an underlying futility of knowing no matter how many you catch, more will escape.

Baehre is unconvinced that any barrier - human, concrete, steel or wire - can stop the Mexicans. Nothing can zip-lock America against illegal immigration. Not when people are hungry enough, poor enough, desperate enough to risk their lives.

"After you're in for a while, you see it's a hopeless situation. You just catch as many as you can," Baehre says.

The illegal immigrants he finds in the fields, construction sites, hotels, restaurants and attractions of Central Florida are the ones who slipped through the net drawn across the Mexican border. There are so many here, there isn't enough money to send them all back.

Of seven illegal Mexicans caught by Baehre and Trevino one morning on their way to a Volusia fernery, two were jailed and five were given 30-day warnings to go back home on their own because the Border Patrol lacks the money to transport them.

"It's like sport fishing on TV," Baehre says. "You catch them and release them."

Both illegal immigrants and Border Patrol agents are engaged in an elaborate, sometimes dangerous, game neither side has any chance of winning. Immigrants are caught and sent back. But the next day there are more, and the game never ends.

You win some, you lose many. But you never keep score.

''You can't think of it as fighting a losing war or you just couldn't come to work any more,'' Baehre says. ''It's your job. You still have to do it no matter what the outcome is.''

On the faces of the young Mexicans caught by Baehre and Trevino, you can see the same acceptance of the inevitable and the same determination to persist.

They look timid, but not intimidated. There is deference in their demeanor, but no fear of deportation.

''They'll tell you, 'We'll be back in three days'," Trevino said.

April 28, 1996

Facing the Future: Time

"It doesn't matter to which God you pray. Precious time is slipping away." (Van Morrison)

Time, as we know it, does not exist at Hyer Street Skool. It doesn't unwind in circles made of seconds, minutes and hours. It doesn't unscroll in days, weeks and years.

To the preschool children dropped off here in the morning and retrieved in the afternoon, time has no meaning except in the ritual of routine and the cycles of nature: nap time, bedtime, daytime, nighttime, spring and summer. They know how many fingers old they are, but have no idea how many days there are between birthdays.

Tyler Wagner believes there are four seconds in a minute, five minutes in an hour, 10 hours in a day and three days before his fifth birthday on July 30.

Kayla Combs is 4 years old and will turn 5 in five minutes.

Tommy Smith says it takes 13 seconds to grow up.

Lindsey White tells time as only a 4-year-old can, announcing throughout the day that it's "line-up time,'' it's "nap time,'' it's "toy time,'' it's "cleanup time.''

The best time, says Brett Forward, whose parents are divorced, is when his father takes him to the park to play.

The longest time, says 3-year-old Katie Duranceau, is waiting to talk to her parents.

The world of preschool is an oasis in time where things move as slowly or as fast as the moment. It is much like the world of our pre-industrial ancestors, when time was something you didn't control, manage, waste, lose or run out of before the end of the day.

"Children live in a more natural time. You try and rush through things with kids and they get really uptight,'' said Alan Hawkins, director of the family studies center at Brigham Young University.

The parents at Hyer Street Skool feel time shrinking, squeezing and condensing as the pace of life seems to accelerate with each generation. And sometimes they wonder, if they can find the time to contemplate, how did life get so hectic? And - if it's bad now - what will it be like when their kids grow up?

Futurists predict that the Hyer Street generation will live better, work less and enjoy more leisure time in the next century. Their parents don't believe it. Americans have been promised the utopia of free time for a hundred years, yet remain enslaved by time now more than ever.

"Never before have we had so little time to do so much." (Franklin D. Roosevelt)

On the cusp of the 20th century, the United States was embroiled in a debate over work hours and leisure time. People were working harder than ever, and there was less time for family, friends and community.

"They were talking about the same things in 1890 that we are talking about now,'' said Benjamin Hunnicutt, a history professor at the University of Iowa. "But overwork in 1890 was thought to be a temporary problem. It would come - the shorter hours would come. Economists predicted it.''

There was good reason for our ancestors to expect that work would retreat in importance and leisure time would expand. Increased productivity from industrialization had reduced the hours Americans were working since 1850, when the average workweek was 70 hours. The promise of more labor-saving devices in the next century assured that the trend would continue.

They need not have worried.

Americans at the end of the 19th century thought that once everyone had the necessities of life, the need for work would diminish. That attitude began to change in the 1920s with the rise of advertising and marketing, which expands the demand for new goods and services. When the Great Depression came in the 1930s, the debate over work and leisure ended, and the issue became how to reduce unemployment. There were two competing ideas.

One, backed by organized labor, was to reduce the workweek to 30 hours, thus providing more jobs for the unemployed. The concept of job-sharing was born in the '30s. The other argument, supported by industry and business, was to create more jobs.

President Franklin Roosevelt initially backed the shorter workweek. A 30-hour workweek bill passed the Senate and seemed certain to pass the House when Roosevelt, bending to business, reversed his position.

Instead of a shorter workweek, Roosevelt proposed a program of government-assisted job creation. It's a strategy that continues today with tax breaks offered to lure new businesses and other government incentives to grow more jobs. Every American community - even those with economies built on tourism and leisure industries - now equates more jobs with progress and prosperity.

"We had the choice and we chose to expand necessity and keep work where it was at 40 hours,'' Hunnicutt said. "We turned our backs on the promised land of leisure.''

The United States became a consumer society with an ever-expanding affluence based on the willingness of Americans to work as long and hard as it takes to maintain the highest standard of living in the world. Trapped inside "capitalism's squirrel cage'' of work-and-spend, Americans are now working 20 more days a year than they were 20 years ago, according to Harvard University economist Juliet Schor, author of The Overworked American. Gone is the idea of a shorter workweek, submerged beneath the need to maintain what we have, or own more.

"In the 19th century, work was widely seen as a means to an end - get enough goods to live on and then move on to the better things in life: family, community and culture,'' Hunnicutt said. "We have lost that vision, and now we are unable to conceive of progressively shorter hours of labor.''

"The secret of your future is hidden in your daily routine." (Mike Murdock)

A red broken heart, left over from a Valentine's Day mural, is painted on the front window of the preschool room at Hyer Street

Skool near downtown Orlando. Kim White opens the window by sliding the heart to one side, then stoops to hug her daughter Lindsey. She pats her child on the back with one hand and clutches her car keys with the other.

"Be good. See you later,'' she says.

At the window, Lindsey waves to the parking lot.

"Bye, Mom,'' she says, and then pushes shut the window.

It's 8:15 a.m., and the classroom is raucous with children playing. There is an order to their day, orchestrated by their teacher, Miss Zeldie, but the activities flow together without the children being aware of the passage of time. The only clock is in the shape of a blue plastic sneaker sitting inconspicuously on the kitchen windowsill. There is no strict regimentation of the day, no concern about keeping kids "on task,'' no time-management techniques to make more out of less, no day-planners and Post-it Notes and pagers clipped to belts.

At 8:51 a.m., when Lindsey, Katie, Tommy, Brett, Tyler and Kayla are learning about Scat the Cat, who changes colors, their parents are logging on to their computers at work, opening mail, listening to voicemail, returning phone calls and checking their e-mail.

At 9:25 a.m., while Kayla Combs is intently trying to tie her shoelace, her father is making phone calls on the way to his job and her mother is composing a memo after finishing breakfast at her desk. On an average day, Donna Combs stops to answer her pager 15 times.

At 12:47 p.m., while Tyler Wagner is asleep in a darkened room with 25 other preschoolers, his mother is checking her voice-mail and e-mail messages for the third time in a day when she will receive more than 70 e-mails and voice-mail recordings.

At 2:44 p.m., when Katie Duranceau is singing "Happy Birthday'' to a girl turning 5, her father is on the phone again - his seventh call in a day of 10 phone conversations.

At 3:36 p.m., while Kristen Forward, an accountant, is filling ledger entries, comparing expenses to budget figures, making spreadsheets and completing a month-end report on her computer, Brett Forward is trying to figure out how to play with another boy's toys without letting go of his own.

At 4:45 p.m., as Lindsey White's dad is loading a malfunctioning fax machine into his car to haul to a repair shop, Lindsey is playing with a toy called My First Laptop.

The parents of Hyer Street Skool move through the day to the measured cadence of clocks. Clock time is objective, calculated and inflexible. Innocent of clock time, the children of Hyer Street experience time from a purely subjective perspective. An hour can pass in a minute, or a minute can seem like an hour. Ask Brett Forward how long a day lasts at Hyer Street Skool and he will tell you.

"A long time," he says. "About 10 years."

"For a nation who has an almost evil reputation for bustle, bustle, bustle and rush, rush, rush, we spend an enormous amount of time standing around in line in front of windows, just waiting." (Robert Benchley)

In the 1300s, the smallest unit of time was the hour. There are still clocks in use in Europe that lack minute and second hands. In 1999, the smallest units of time are so small they are imperceptible. Computers run on nanoseconds - one-billionth of a second - and are becoming faster all the time.

The influence is almost insidious, but computers are altering our sense of time. In clock time, everything moves at the same speed, one second at a time. In the digital world of cyberspace, everything moves so fast that time ceases to exist.

"The more we operate in virtual environments, the more we see time not as fixed - as the clock taught us - but as fluid and programmable," said Richard Rogers, assistant professor of communications at Northern Arizona University.

Think of computer games where difficulty is determined by speed. Each level is faster than the one before it. The winner is not someone who finishes the game in the shortest amount of time, but who most closely matches the speed of the computer.

Wayne Smith, Tommy's dad, escapes time stress by submerging himself inside the clockless world of computer games.

"Time flies, absolutely flies when I'm playing computer

games,'' Smith said. "You don't care about time. You just tune out the world.''

You don't need to understand a nanosecond to feel its effect: It's the irritation computer users get when it takes more than a split-second for a function to perform. It's the frustration people feel inside their cars when stuck in traffic. The impatience of waiting for the fast food to arrive. The antsy feeling while watching the seconds tick backward on the microwave.

"When you increase the pace, you increase impatience,'' said social critic Jeremy Rifkin, author of Time Wars. "When you increase impatience, you have a loss of civility, a loss of empathy, a loss of community.''

The faster pace of life not only creates impatience, but makes relaxation more difficult. Free time becomes another vessel to fill, not a flower to smell.

"I very rarely even sit down and watch TV,'' said Kim White, Lindsey's mother. "If I sit down for a couple of minutes, I remember something I should be doing.''

For children raised on the nanosecond, the high-tech pace of life also produces a difficulty staying focused on any one thing for very long.

"We have a generation of young people with very, very short attention spans. We have children who can't compose a sentence because learning to read and write moves too slow for them,'' Rifkin said.

The time deficit so many people experience spreads across society. It has been blamed for increasing sleep disorders, declining civic involvement, lower voter turnout and falling membership in social, fraternal and volunteer organizations. In response to feeling time-squeezed, Americans try "time-deepening'' techniques that actually contribute to the feeling of being rushed, according to sociologists John P. Robinson and Geoffrey Godbey, authors of Time for Life: The Surprising Ways Americans Use Their Time.

"Sometimes you're cooking dinner and answering your messages and opening your mail and unloading the dishwasher while feeding the kids and doing some laundry,'' said Donna Combs, Kayla's mother.

The ironic result of "time-deepening'' is that it produces a more shallow life. Living a busier life, we skim across the surface of our existence by avoiding or eliminating the things that take time.

"Starving for time does not result in death, but in never beginning to live,'' contend the authors of Time for Life. "Instead of time-saving skills, we need to cultivate life-savoring skills."

"The trouble with our times is that the future is not what it used to be." (Paul Valery)

On the cusp of the 21st century, futurists predict a world familiar to historians: High-tech advances in the next 20-25 years will create a quantum leap in productivity and a decline in the hours of work.

"Very early in the next century, by 2010, we will be able to produce all the services and goods with 70 percent of the work force,'' said James Coates, who heads a future research firm in Washington, D.C. "We'll see extended vacations, shorter workweeks, shorter work lives.''

There is one significant difference, however, between predictions of a shorter workweek in the 21st century and the same expectations in 1899: There is no widespread assumption that increased productivity will result in more leisure time and less work.

Among the parents of Hyer Street Skool children, the presumption is that the pace of life will get faster, and their children will be working as long and hard - if not longer and harder - than they are.

"I heard that by 2020, the workweek will be cut down to three days,'' said Debbie Wagner, Tyler's mom. "I don't believe it. I don't see it happening. I think it will get worse.''

In the past, labor unions carried the banner for less work and more leisure. No such movement exists at the end of the '90s. Exiting the squirrel cage of work-and-spend consumerism is possible when individuals make a conscious choice to trade money for time. They simplify their lives, curtail their desires, pass up promotions, buy smaller houses, drive older cars, eschew credit cards. But those people swim against the flow of American culture.

"I'm an optimist," said Hawkins, the BYU family studies director. "I think we will see a class of worker emerge over the next 30 years that will be more family-centered, that will be more balanced."

Historian Hunnicutt counters that it would take an unprecedented shift in how Americans view time, work and leisure for future generations to reclaim control of the clock.

"If shorter work hours are seen as a progressive phenomenon - my generation worked eight-hour days, my children's generation will work six-hour days - that would be a historical change," Hunnicutt said. "I don't see it on the horizon."

"Work is a fine thing if it doesn't take too much of your spare time." (Anonymous)

Kayla Combs' mother, Donna, pulls into the Hyer Street Skool parking lot at 4:55 p.m. in a white Ford Explorer with a license plate that reads "Outtatime." She wears a pager on a cord around her neck. It takes her five minutes to fetch Kayla and her 2-year-old sister, Sarah, strap them into their car seats and head for swimming lessons.

She puts the kids to bed at 8:10 p.m., and her husband, Mark, puts them back to bed at 9 p.m. After the kids fall asleep, Donna will fold clothes as she watches TV. Mark will read a cooking magazine while watching a country-music awards show.

After Katie Duranceau's dad picks her up, he will retrieve her 6-year-old brother, Matt, from school, bathe the kids and feed them pizza before attending a two-hour school advisory meeting. After putting the children to bed at 9:45 p.m., he will go downstairs to work until 10:15 p.m.

Lindsey White's mom will pull into Hyer Street at 5:07 p.m. and pick up Kentucky Fried Chicken for supper. Her husband, Jim, will pick up their 7-year-old son Kyle from school at 5:20 p.m. They will rendezvous at home, eat and head out together for Kyle's baseball game at 6 p.m.

Tommy Smith's mother will stop on the way home from the

preschool to buy supplies for his sister Samantha's first birthday, feed and bathe the kids, put Samantha to bed, take out the trash, wash the dishes, balance the checkbook, eat dinner, put Tommy to bed, clean the house, call her husband, who is out of town, spend a half-hour getting things ready for the next workday, watch a little TV and go to bed at 10 p.m.

Each parent has forsaken something to the 24-hour day. They have given up reading, exercise, sleep, solitude and relaxation.

"Leisure time just for myself - that's something I just don't have anymore," said Bonnie Duranceau, Katie's mom.

Some have carved little islands of time for themselves. Kim White gets up a half-hour early in the morning to take a walk. Kristen Forward, a single mom, exercises on her lunch hour.

Patty Smith, Tommy's mom, has roped off her home life to create a sanctuary from work: "I've stopped bringing work home. I've just drawn the line."

Throughout time, each generation has followed the footsteps of its ancestors. Standing on the edge of the next millennium, we must wonder where we are leading our descendants.

"Whether we are going to be these time slaves 20 or 30 years from now is one of the most significant questions we need to be asking," Alan Hawkins said. "I really don't think people enjoy this. I think there will be an adjustment, but sometimes it takes a generation or two."

May 31, 1999

WATERSHED

FAMU: A March to Tragedy

It's 7 p.m. on Aug. 22, 2011. A thunderstorm is passing through Tallahassee as 350 members of the Florida A&M University Marching 100 assemble for the first time inside the school's cavernous band-rehearsal hall.

The students are seated in a semicircle of padded orange chairs on the green-carpeted floor -- all dressed as if attending church. Behind them high on a wall, looking over their shoulders, is the portrait of the legendary William P. Foster, clad in white, who founded and made famous the Marching 100.

It's the first time freshmen and upperclassmen have been together as a band, seated by section, arranged by instruments: clarinets, piccolos, French horns, saxophones, trumpets, trombones, tubas, drums.

The freshmen are coming off one week of drills to teach them the basics of marching band: steps, movements, routines, music. It's their first taste of what the semester will bring: long, exacting practices on the open field they call "the Patch" and the initiation ritual of hazing. They've already been scolded and taunted by the upperclass band members, warned never to walk on the patch. Freshmen don't deserve to walk. They have to run across the grass.

Before them are longtime band director Julian E. White; his nine-member staff; and an array of high-profile officials, students and alumni: FAMU President James Ammons, the director of the university police department, the president of the student government and the head of the band-alumni association. Off to one side are the six drum majors, all dressed alike and arranged by height.

The drum majors represent the pinnacle of achievement in the Marching 100: the student field generals of one of the nation's most celebrated marching bands. Among that group, Robert Champion -- poised to become the head drum major the following year -- is hard to miss.

He's a big guy, 26 years old, a little more than 6 feet tall and 235 pounds. He is remarkable in a number of ways. He's gay and doesn't hide it. He appeared as a teenager in the 2002 movie

"Drumline," loosely based on the FAMU band. More importantly, he has managed to move up the ranks, for the most part, without subjecting himself to the semester-long hazing that faces the freshmen seated before him.

Hazing is the reason they are all assembled. Since 1998, the university has held hazing workshops to drill into the heads of the band students that hazing is unacceptable, hazing is against school regulations, hazing is against the law.

The university has good reason to beat the drum. Ivery Luckey, a clarinetist, was hospitalized for two weeks after being paddled more than 300 times in 1998. Trumpeter Marcus Parker went into renal failure following a 2001 hazing. Luckey won a $50,000 settlement. Parker was awarded $1.8 million in his lawsuit against the band members who beat him.

Speaker after speaker -- Ammons, White, campus-police Chief Calvin Ross -- repeat the same mantra: Participating in hazing, either as a victim or a hazer, can cost you your music scholarship. You can be expelled from school. You can be arrested and charged with a third-degree felony.

In the workshop, band members hear that hazing extends beyond physical abuse. It includes doing chores and running errands for upperclassmen; extorting money from freshmen; and demeaning and abusive language.

Marcus Fabre', seated in the saxophone section, knows from experience the gap between what the adults say and what happens inside the band. He's a 20-year-old sophomore who spent his freshman year refusing to be hazed and paying the price with ostracism. The upperclassmen used him as an example: If you don't submit, you'll end up alone, just like Marcus.

There are others inside the rehearsal hall for whom the anti-hazing warnings are hollow admonishments and empty threats. Some of them belong to small groups within the sections: clarinetists who call themselves the "Clones," trumpet players who go by "Thunder," and a group of students from Georgia called the "Red Dawg Order."

They know hazing is banned but are determined to perpetuate it. Within six months, 26 of them will be suspended from performing at the Florida Classic football game in Orlando for hazing. Seven will be arrested.

In the final act of the hazing workshop, all band members sign a "hazing and harassment agreement" that acknowledges participating "as a hazer or hazee will immediately terminate my membership in the band."

As one band member signs the pledge, he thinks: They're going to do it anyway.

In another row, a freshman signs the document with little thought to the promise he's making. "Nobody took it seriously," he said.

That would become obvious within three short months as the band marched blindly toward tragedy.

Life in the Band

In early September, days after the hazing workshop, five "pledges" line up according to height before members of the Clones, the clarinet subgroup. Inside the off-campus home of two Clones, the pledges begin their initiation into the group. They are exercised past the point of exhaustion and made to perform music to the strict satisfaction of upperclassmen. They are punched, slapped, paddled and belittled with profane insults. At least one leaves the hazing with bruises on her buttocks.

One pledge, Shantivia Conley, has had enough. When she doesn't return for the second hazing, the others are "prepped" -- slapped hard on the back with two hands -- for allowing Conley to quit. One is ordered to prep Conley for not showing up for further hazing.

In subsequent hazings, the four remaining pledges are extorted for money by the Clones, beaten, demeaned and pushed to exhaustion. It's the pain and indignity some FAMU students are willing to endure to win acceptance into the most famous college marching band in the country.

The legend of the Marching 100 draws students from throughout Florida and across the nation to the historically black university in Tallahassee: kids from Orlando, Miami, Jacksonville, Tallahassee, but also Atlanta, Detroit and Chicago.

This is the band that starred in television commercials, marched in presidential inaugurations, performed at Super Bowl halftimes, played with Kanye West at the Grammy Awards and was featured on "60 Minutes."

Everywhere band members go, from campus to the courthouse to the DoubleTree Hotel in downtown Tallahassee, they see pictures of the famous FAMU bands of the past. For some, this is the realization of the dream they had in high school. For others, a band scholarship to FAMU is their only way to attend college. About half the band is on scholarship or receiving financial aid.

Many are music majors, but some are not. They plan to pursue careers in business, pharmacy, law and education, but for now they are willing to sacrifice for the glory of belonging to the "Incomparable Marching 100, World's Best."

They are young men and women, many away from home for the first time, with the need for acceptance and belonging. The most vulnerable are willing to do just about anything -- endure pain, risk their scholarships -- to make it inside the secret and select subgroups of the Clones, Thunder, Gestapo, Red Dawgs, Screaming Demons, B Tone Express, Whales and The Z.

But this is not the kind of hazing students endured in some high-school bands -- silly stuff such as forcing a boy to wear a bra on the outside of his shirt or making a girl wear a "kick me" sign to class.

As in the military, the youngest recruits endure taunts on the practice field meant to break their spirit or force them to work harder. Go kill yourself, freshman. Why are you here? Women are insulted with sexist slurs. Male freshmen are made to feel emasculated, ignored as if they don't exist, when they try to talk to upperclassmen.

Freshmen are forced to remain together at all times. Eat together. Arrive for practice together. Walk your freshman sister to class. When they travel to football games and other events, they're bullied and made to turn over the money they receive to pay for their meals.

In text messages and phone calls, upperclassmen order them to provide everything from candy and sports drinks to liquor and a barbecue grill.

Sometimes, when a student doesn't know his music or plays a wrong note, he's hit with the bell of a horn or punched in the arm.

The long hours of practice in the hot Florida sun -- from 3:30 p.m. to as late as 7 p.m. Monday through Friday -- make it tough. The hard work, paired with the constant degradation, makes some feel like quitting virtually every day.

"Everything made you want to quit," said a freshman who stuck it out.

Hazing predators and their willful victims were there when Bernie Hendricks was in the band from 1991-97. They were probably there, too, when his father was in the band from 1958 to 1963. Hendricks' father was director of student activities from 1986 until his death in 1992, and one of his duties was to suspend and expel band members caught hazing.

When Bernie joined the band as a drummer, his father warned him against hazing: "If you do something, I'll have to kick you out of school, just like I've had to kick other kids out of school."

But the line is sometimes blurry between what constitutes hazing and what is part of the military-like drills, discipline and precision that go into becoming the best marching band. A section leader may yell at a trombone player for missing a note, or an upperclassman may belittle a freshman for failing to master a complicated drill step. Are those acts of hazing or expressions of what it takes to make it in the Marching 100?

"It's not for everybody," said Hendricks, 38, the band director at Ocoee High School. "It's a big commitment, and some can't handle it so they quit and use that [hazing] as an excuse."

That gradation of what constitutes hazing leaves it up to every band member to decide what he or she is willing to do, and where to draw the line. Jason Lawrence, who played clarinet from 2007-09 along with Robert Champion, never considered verbal harassment an act of hazing, but he drew the line at physical contact. Nobody was going to put their hands on him -- and nobody did.

"People only go through what they allow someone to do to

them," said Lawrence, 22, who graduated in 2011.

The roughest, most physical hazing takes place off campus -- often late at night. Students have to find a ride to get there and then find their way home afterward.

Timothy Barber, a former head drum major who graduated in 2002, drew his line at the end of practice. He didn't hang with upperclassmen. He didn't go to their dorms or apartments after hours. He didn't meet them on the practice field after midnight.

But he, too, heard the competing voices. They came from alumni who reminded everyone in the band how easy students had it now. Today's band was not as good, not as accomplished, not as tough as those illustrious bands of the past.

And Barber, 37, heard the voices of upperclassmen saying hazing is the tradition of the band, it's what builds camaraderie, it's the fire in the forge that makes us stronger.

"Who are you going to listen to? You have students coming into the FAMU band and these underground sources saying you have to do it because these people did it," said Barber. "You don't have enough people saying, 'It didn't happen to me, so you shouldn't let it happen to you,' or 'It happened to me, and it was wrong.' "

Not enough voices, speaking loudly enough from within the band itself, saying hazing isn't what makes the band great. It's the marching and the music, nothing else.

Humiliation and assaults are not humbling -- they are harmful.

"They call it 'humblizing,' " said Marcus Fabre'. "But humble doesn't mean getting hit and not doing anything about it. It means you are willing to learn, and you don't know everything. Paddling doesn't help you do anything better."

Warning Signs

On Oct. 31, inside an off-campus apartment, 18-year-old Bria Hunter is being berated for trying to skip a meeting of the Red Dawg Order. Hunter, a freshman clarinetist, is from the same Atlanta-area high school as Robert Champion. Champion tells Hunter she doesn't need to subject herself to hazing. She ignores him, but after enduring physical abuse during Red Dawg meetings, Hunter has second thoughts.

Inside that apartment with about 11 other pledges, she is punished for telling a lie to skip the initiation meeting. For lying, she is forced to march in place while two of the other Red Dawg members beat her on the legs with their fists.

Hunter is 5-feet-1 and weighs 112 pounds. The two Red Dawgs beating on her legs are 6-feet-3, about 175 pounds, and 5-feet-8, 150 pounds. One is 19, the other 23.

The next day, the Red Dawgs repeat the treatment, this time using a metal ruler across the top of Hunter's thighs. The beatings cause blood clots in her legs, deep bone bruises and a broken femur. On Nov. 7, unable to stand the pain, Bria Hunter is taken to the hospital by ambulance.

Within a few days, Band Director Julian White suspends 26 band members from participating in the Florida Classic for hazing.

As word of Hunter's injuries and the suspensions spread through the band, Fabre' remembers his attempts to convince freshmen members that they didn't need to be hazed.

You can be in the band without submitting to the abuse, he told them.

Yeah, but look at what happened to you, they responded: You're shunned, you're all alone.

But if you all stand up to hazing, you won't be alone. You'll all be together, he replied.

"I tried to get the other freshmen to stand up," Fabre' said. "Nobody wanted to be in my shoes."

The injury to Hunter and the suspensions should have been the warning sign that things have gone too far, the tradition is off the tracks. This is Ivery Luckey and Marcus Parker all over again.

Instead of backing off, the FAMU hazers stand defiant and undeterred.

They would prove true the prophecy by the mother of Fabre'. Earlier in the semester, she met with Julian White about the harassment of her son for refusing to be hazed.

"If you don't do more to stop this, somebody is going to get killed," Felicia Fabre' said.

Aboard Bus C

On the afternoon of Nov. 19, Orlando's Florida Citrus Bowl fills with 60,000 spectators for the 66th meeting of the Florida A&M University Rattlers and the Bethune-Cookman University Wildcats.

They are here -- dividing the stadium into opposite sides of green and orange, gold and maroon -- ostensibly to watch a football game, but really to watch the halftime battle of the bands. The Classic -- a "show interrupted by a football game" -- is where everybody goes to the bathroom before halftime, not during.

By the time the FAMU band takes the field, led by Robert Champion and the five other drum majors, the sky is turning dark as storm clouds move over the stadium.

For the freshmen in the Marching 100, making it to the Florida Classic is all that matters. It's the last performance of the football season, and band members are treated like celebrities.

Their nine buses are escorted by Orlando Police Department motorcycles from the Rosen Plaza hotel to the Citrus Bowl. Bus A, the lead bus where the band staff and section leaders ride, is the most luxurious ride -- complete with a sunroof, wood floors and electrical outlets at every seat. Julian White and the drum majors ride to the game in a black limousine.

After the Classic, win or lose, the band rejoices. A collective relief comes with the end of months of practice, the striving for perfection, the precision necessary to master the 360-steps-per-minute re-enactment of a rattlesnake's strike.

Upperclassmen are hugging and congratulating freshmen. They're exchanging gifts and personal items, including band hats and jackets. Hazers and hazees, tormentors and victims, are now good friends.

One freshman was prepared to confront the upperclassmen who had bullied him, but after the Classic, he was greeted "like when a soldier comes back and the family rushes at you."

"My goal was to not change ..., but you can't help it," he said. "After I thought about it, I was kind of like, 'I was being over-dramatic a lot of the times. It really wasn't that bad.' "

In that one moment, the torment is forgotten and forgiven. And sometimes, in that instant, a hazee begins the transition into a hazer, perpetuating the tradition upon the next class of freshmen.

"Abused children become abusers," Felicia Fabre' said. "That is what happens with the band: Abused band members become abusers."

For many of the freshmen in the Marching 100, the Florida Classic is the end of the abuse. But not for those who ride back to the Rosen Plaza hotel aboard Bus C.

Marcus Fabre' knows all about Bus C. In his freshman year, when he was being ostracized for refusing to be hazed, he found his name listed on Bus C after the Classic. He knew he didn't belong on that bus, which carries mostly members of the percussion section. He knew he was being set up.

"They tried to get me on that bus last year," Fabre' said. "I just didn't ride it."

The percussion subgroup, called The Z, has its own initiation ritual that takes place throughout the semester. It's called "Crossing Bus C." And it would cost Robert Champion his life.

After the game, the charter buses are escorted back to the hotel. Bus C parks in the back of the hotel, the engine running. About 30 FAMU band members are aboard the bus.

A number of students subject themselves to hazing. Some will walk from the front to the back of the bus while being attacked. Sometimes, the hazing victim sits in the "hot seat" at the back of the bus while being slapped and beaten.

Nobody knows why Robert Champion boarded Bus C. The bus he rode from Tallahassee to Orlando was Bus H. Some students speculate that, after years of resisting hazing and warning others not to participate, Champion decided to submit to earn the respect and loyalty of the band before he became head drum major the following year. The Classic would be his last chance at acceptance. Others suggest he might have been lured inside the bus and beaten as his punishment for his stance against hazing.

Tall, heavy-set, with a shaved head and a short-cropped

beard and mustache, Robert Champion moves down the narrow aisle between the rows of seats through a gauntlet of fists.

He is struck in the stomach, arms, chest and back. One purplish-gray bruise extends from the top of his back almost to his waist. Beneath those bruises and abrasions, his body is bleeding.

Immediately after the beating, Champion complains of thirst and exhaustion. His vision blurs, he vomits and collapses inside the bus.

Holding Champion as he is dying, an unidentified person calls 911 at 9:46 p.m.

"He is in my hands, ma'am. He's cold. He's in my hands," the male says. "His eyes are open, but he's not responding."

About an hour later, Robert Champion dies in Dr. P. Phillips Hospital. Early the next day, Julian White identifies the body.

The cause of death is listed as hemorrhagic shock caused by blunt-force trauma: killed by hazing.

Here is what else died that day: the shiny-brass reputation of a precision college marching band.

The famous FAMU band is suffering from a self-inflicted wound by a cadre of band members who believed they were untouchable, beyond reproach and superior in their conceit that nothing bad would happen. Until it did.

Since Robert Champion's death

Four FAMU students, Hakeem Birch, Denise Bailey, Anthony Mingo and Brandon Benson, have been charged with a misdemeanor for the hazing of the five clarinet Clone pledges. Three other students, James Harris, Aaron Golson and Sean Hobson, have been arrested on charges of hazing Bria Hunter. Golson and Hobson were also charged with felony battery.

On Jan. 11, FAMU campus police issued a year-long, campus-wide trespass warning against a band student accused of harassing another student to join the Thunder subgroup.

Two months after the death of Robert Champion, the hazing continues.

February 5, 2012

Faces and Places: Disaster

A few vacant lots where houses once stood are the last reminders of the killer tornado that ripped through the Hyde Park mobile-home community four years ago this Friday.

Three people in the Winter Garden retirement community were among 42 Central Florida residents killed by a series of tornadoes that swept through the center of the state, ripping up subdivisions and mobile-home parks.

Disasters -- tornadoes, hurricanes, fires, floods, even terrorism attacks -- destroy places, but in their immediate wake, they create the true meaning of community.

In the minutes after the tornado hit Hyde Park on Feb. 22, 1998, there were neighbors meeting for the first time, people helping people, strangers befriending strangers.

"Everybody was pitching in to help. They were looking after each other," said John Harriman, 72, former homeowner-association president.

On Hyde Park Circle, across the street from empty Lot 130, Ed White took four people into his home, including two neighbors he had never met before. Next door to Lot 130, Helen Montgomery collected phone numbers from survivors so she would call family members and tell them their relatives were all right or on the way to the hospital.

On Royal View Circle, a stranger from down the street comforted Carol Cox after she was helped down from the roof of a neighbor's house where she and her husband Bill landed when their home was lifted into the air and blown to pieces.

The same disaster dynamic was found in New York when office workers risked their lives to help strangers down the stairs of the World Trade Center. And in the acts of heroism and compassion after Hurricane Andrew flattened Homestead in 1992. And the Oklahoma City bombing in 1995.

Wherever disaster strikes, community is created. But then, just like the disasters that spawned them, that intense sense of community disappears.

"I have a brother in Oklahoma City who said that after the bombing, people would walk up and talk to you, and you didn't know half of them," said Hyde Park resident Norma Jordan, 66. "After a couple of years, it was back to normal. You're right back to where it was before."

Disasters have a way of peeling away the routine of daily life to reveal, amid all the sorrow and destruction, what truly makes us human.

"When we experience this involvement with others, I think we feel our humanity," said Alan Lipton, Florida director for Magellan Behavioral Health Care, which provides mental-health services.

Crises can even penetrate psychosis, reaching beyond mental illness to the core of human caring for others in danger. At a San Francisco mental institution rocked by a 1971 earthquake, a patient who had been admitted hours before with a mental illness so severe that he had to be put in restraints, helped an 18-year-old catatonic girl evacuate the hospital. Within hours, he retreated back inside his illness.

Disaster psychologists describe the transformation that takes place after a tragedy as the "community of sufferers." All the things that normally estrange neighbors from one another disappear in a disaster, as if torn into pieces and carried away by the wind. Replacing the petty disputes over dog poop and loud parties is the intense, common experience of having survived a life-threatening situation.

"One of the things that promotes a sense of community is when people have shared values that supersede any other values. That's what comes to the foreground in times of crisis," said Mary Beth Kenkel, dean of psychology at the Florida Institute of Technology in Melbourne. "Another thing that happens in crisis is people are more likely to ask for help, which again promotes a sense of community."

Just as tornadoes rip away walls to reveal what's inside a person's house, disasters also open people to sharing thoughts, feelings and fears they wouldn't normally confide. An intimacy that didn't exist before the disaster is left behind after the danger departs.

"People feel more vulnerable so they are open to new ideas, new ways of behaving, new ways of thinking," Kenkel said. "But if nothing is actually done differently, that sense of belonging fades into the background."

For places with stable populations, disasters become part of the fabric of the community transferred to those who didn't experience the event. The event becomes part of the place's history and its identity -- linking one generation to another and newcomers with old-timers.

But the community-building effect of disasters is usually short-lived -- even more so when the place has an ever-changing population. Along with the drive to rebuild comes the desire to return to normal.

If the one thing that brought people together is the disaster itself, there comes a time when neighbors no longer want to discuss the disaster. And when that happens, they go back to having as much, or as little, in common as they had before the crisis.

"It's the events that draw them together that they don't want to talk about any more; they don't want to talk about the only thing they have in common," said Rocky Lopes, associate for disaster education at the American Red Cross in Washington.

Routine reasserts itself and the closeness that exists after the disaster slowly dissipates.

"As time goes on, the old problems come back. And not only the old problems, but additional problems created by the relief effort," said E.L. Quarantelli, former director of the Disaster Research Center at the University of Delaware.

In New York, the return to normalcy started with the competing complaints that survivors were not receiving enough compensation from government and relief agencies.

In Hyde Park, the tornado trauma has receded behind new concerns -- such as opposition to plans by the Publix next door to move across State Road 50.

"At the time, everybody was willing to help everybody else out. People let other people move in with them. People were friendly -- `If you need help, let me know. If you need a ride, anything,' " Norma Jordan said. "It lasted maybe the first year. After that, it's the same."

The mobile-home park residents held a service

commemorating the first anniversary of the tornado and then sat down together to eat a potluck dinner. But there was no such gathering the next year.

"A lot of people here don't even want to be reminded of it -- especially those who had a lot of damage," said Bob Bakker, 67, the Hyde Park homeowners association president. "They don't even want to think about it."

Some residents mark the anniversary in their minds whenever Feb. 22 rolls around. But for others in the park, the date means nothing. With 475 houses and 600 residents, Hyde Park has about 30 homes for sale at any one time. Neighbors die, move to nursing homes or return to their home states to be with their children. New people move in and, except for the empty lots, see nothing that suggests this place was torn apart by a tornado late one night four years ago.

"These new people who moved in will say, `Well, you've never had any bad storms here have you?' And I'll think, `Oh, my God, you're living on the space where people died,' '' said Helen Montgomery, 73.

Disaster experts contend that even after the "community of sufferers" disappears, something indelible is left behind. It may be a subterranean sense of community, but disaster survivors are more likely to help each other in the future than they were in the past.

"We still hear of people who met as the result of a disaster who are still caring for one another, still looking after each other," Lopes said. "It happens over time that people begin to return to their normal routines, but it doesn't go all the way back to zero."

Helen Montgomery feels the tornado has changed her. Before the storm, she was steadfast in her independence. If she needed something, she took care of it herself. Now, she feels there is a silent, standing offer of assistance between neighbors that didn't exist before.

"I would ask for help now, and I know I would get it. And I would give it, too," she said.

You can't tell by looking that Montgomery's house had been riddled by rocks, lost part of its roof and had shards of window glass sticking into the walls like a dartboard. Everything has been repaired and put back into place. The only souvenir she kept from the tornado is a bedroom alarm clock. She cut off the cord and set it on a shelf in her living room beside her daughter's wedding photo and a crystal apple from her days as a teacher.

The hands of the clock are forever frozen at 11:46 p.m., the exact minute a tornado tore apart a mobile-home park and built a community.

February 18, 2002

Adam Walsh: Slaying Puts City on Guard

HOLLYWOOD, Fla – As the two women push through the Sears entrance that faces the police station, one says to the other, "Where was it that little boy got grabbed?"

Straight ahead. Past the men's clothing. At the corner of two broad aisles in the lamp department on the right, where Reve Walsh shopped while her son played about 25 yards away with the computer and video games at the toy department's family game center.

It's Thursday, 17 days since Adam Walsh disappeared. Three days since his head was recovered from the canal. Women walk though the store with the hands of their children locked in their own.

A mother admonishes her son, "Stay close." She guides him to the catalog counter, 5 feet from the TV with the video games on its screen. The boy's eyes fix on the TV. His feet inch closer to it.

"Nick!" says his mother, sternly. "Where are you supposed to be? I'm not over there. Stay with me."

A few minutes later, Mrs. Mac Gruber pulls her four grandchildren, aged 7 to 2, into the toy department. The children are tied together with black bailing twine.

"I'm up-tight because some nut might snatch my kids," she says. "I used to flip in and out of here like nothing. I used to just hold their hands and let them go. And now I have them tied up.

"They're most unhappy being tied together."

As she tugs the kids past 18-year-old store clerk Linda Schainberg, Mrs. Gruber says, "You think I'm crazy, don't you?"

"No, I don't," Mrs. Schainberg says. She understands perfectly the queasy feeling people carry around inside when they walk down the aisles of this or any other Hollywood department store. She feels it too.

She's afraid to have a child in South Florida. She and her husband of nearly a year decided, before the Adam Walsh tragedy, that they'll move from Hollywood before they start their family.

Maybe they'll go to a small town somewhere. To a place where the children are safe.

But where is that?

Despite the extra precautions of twine and tighter grips, kids still get separated from their parents. Being children, they like to hide in the clothing racks when their parents turn their backs.

And then, even while the terror of Adam Walsh's gruesome death is still fresh in parental minds, a voice comes over the department store public address system:

"We have a little boy who is missing..."

***

The Sears department store where Adam Walsh was kidnapped is framed in the windows of Hollywood police Lt. Richard Hynds' third-story office.

Looking directly across traffic-clogged Hollywood Boulevard at the Hollywood Mall, Hynds sees the red Sears sign every morning when he walks into his office. It's like a taunt, an unwavering reminder that the crime that has launched the largest manhunt in South Florida happened, literally, beneath Richard Hynds' nose.

"Had I been looking that way, I would have seen the incident," said Hynds, who leads the search to find the 6-year-old boy's killer.

Hynds hunts 18 hours a day. He has a good idea of what the man looks like and the kind of vehicle he drives. Moreover, he knows the kind of killer he is after: "We're dealing with some kind of criminal psychopath who might have done this kind of thing before. He needs to be apprehended before he does it again."

The killer has an unlikely adversary in Hynds – a 51-year-old former Buffalo, N.Y., plumber who has been in law enforcement for 25 years.

Hynds looks like Captain Kangaroo with a handlebar mustache. A robust, heavy-set man with a chubby face and gray-tinted hair combed straight forward, Hynds became commander of the 32-man detective division about 18 months ago after serving as a motorcycle cop and head of the traffic and communications division.

Yet, there is no doubt in Hynds' mind that he will catch Adam's murderer.

“This will take a lot of leg work, but we're going to get him eventually,” Hynds said.

He has plenty of help, from the six detectives working full time with him, a myriad of other cooperating law enforcement agencies, and the people who keep the department telephones ringing with tips, suspicions and new clues.

A police officer logs the telephone calls on a yellow legal note pad. Someone calls about a suspicious trash bag, a sack of garbage too neatly tied to contain just refuse. A psychic calls with the premonition that the rest of Adam's body will be found near water. The telephone log is turned over to a detective sergeant who decides which tips should be followed up and which should be discarded.

“Something will turn up somewhere. The little key will give us a clue to his identity. One of these little leads will be the one,” Hynds said.

The $100,000 reward offered by an anonymous donor for the capture of the killer may help turn up that little key, Hynds said. Or maybe it will come from someone close to the murderer who realizes he needs help or another child might die.

“There might be someone close to him who may come forward to get help for this person,” Hynds said. “The possibility is good that he might never go to trial, he's so sick.”

The most promising lead investigators have is the description given by a 10-year-old Hollywood boy who saw the suspected killer drive by the Sears store in a blue van. The Hollywood youth saw a van pull alongside Adam outside the Sears store, stop, and a door open. When the van left, Adam also was gone. But until his family agreed to have their son hypnotized, he could not provide a detailed description of the van or the abductor.

Based on the description supplied by the boy, Hynds believes that the killer is a white man in his mid-20s; between 5 feet 10 inches and 6 feet; 180 to 200 pounds, with a muscular build; curly, styled dark brown or black hair; and a mustache.

He probably lives in South Florida, is most likely still in the state and drives a late model (1979-81) Navy blue Ford van with Florida license plates, black front bumper, a chrome ladder on the left rear, no spare wheel on the back, mag wheels, tinted windows and a rectangular window on the sliding door of the passenger side.

The search for the killer is centered on finding the blue van, beginning with a list of all Ford vans sold in South Florida in the past couple of years.

The other effort is directed toward finding the body of Adam, whose head was recovered from an Indian River County canal off Florida's Turnpike about two weeks after his kidnapping. If the body is found, it may offer a clue to the identity of the killer or lead to the weapon used in the murder.

Hynds theorizes that if the rest of the body, or its parts, were tossed into the water, they would have surfaced before the head. He believes that the mutilation was done inside the van or a building and that the rest of the body is in the South Florida area.

But until some solid tip is received about where to look in the Hollywood area, the search continues along the turnpike and its feeder roads. The hunt is being conducted with help from the Florida Game and Fresh Water Commission, the Florida Highway Patrol, the Indian River County Sheriff's Department and civilian volunteers.

A highway patrolman reported that he saw a blue van parked along the turnpike about 9 miles south of where Adam's head was found, but the van had left before he could turn his cruiser around.

Assistance from the FBI has helped by making its sophisticated crime-analysis equipment available and may be used further to draw up a personality profile of the killer. But, Hynds said, the FBI isn't the crime cure-all many people believe it to be.

"The FBI can't wave a magic wand and have magical things happen. They can't put the manpower on the streets, while we can."

Most of the 400-person Hollywood Police Department has been involved in one way or another with the search for Adam and his killer, said detective Capt. Bob Mowers.

The Hollywood detectives also are thumbing through 6,000 tickets issues on the turnpike in the two weeks before Adam's body was found. If necessary, Hynds said, they will fingerprint all the toll receipts issued that time.

No attempts has been made to hypnotize the tollkeepers, however, because like the Sears store clerks, none of the toll collectors recalls seeing anything that might be helpful.

"That's practically valueless. What kind of scrutiny do you get from toll takers? We don't put much hope in it," he said.

Hynds said it would require hypnotizing all of the tollkeepers on duty, at all the toll exits, the first four days after the kidnapping, because the Broward County medical examiner estimates that Adam was killed within four days of his abduction.

Police are no longer actively looking for a woman who was believed to have been seen with Adam at a miniature golf course because it's likely that Adam was already dead at the time of the sighting, Hynds said.

Hollywood police also have checked out and discarded the possibility that the crime was committed by an associate of Adam's parents, John and Reve Walsh.

One of the reasons the Adam Walsh abduction and macabre murder have drawn such wide sympathy from people throughout the nation is that John and Reve Walsh are a young, personable, middle-class couple with whom people can easily identify.

The Walshes live on a lazy residential street within earshot of children playing on a nearby elementary school playground. Their home is in the less-than-$100,000 price range, a simple, white concrete block and red brick affair, three bedrooms, two baths, a nicely landscaped front yard of shade trees, weeping willows, pines and palms, fenced-in back yard and one-car garage.

Outside the garage sits a tricycle.

For John and Reve Walsh, the agony is over. Adam, the little boy his parents said was too good for this world, is gone.

A Mass of the Angels was celebrated for Adam on Saturday morning at St. Maurice Catholic Church in Hollywood.

By establishing the Adam Walsh Memorial Fund, with $120,000 already collected, the Walshes have shifted their effort toward helping families whose children are still missing.

Nationwide, there are 22 organizations searching for missing children, but they are largely shoe-string operations without the financial resources that may become available through the Walsh fund. The Walshes also plan to lobby for the Child Awareness Act in Congress.

August 1, 1981

Columbia Disaster: Heart of a Tragedy

HEMPHILL, Texas -- In front of L & B Auto Repair, where Farm Road 83 meets State Highway 87, there's a white, concrete Texas-sized star on a circular field of blue.

In this place where Columbia fell from the sky, the newly minted landmark has become a makeshift shrine to the space-shuttle crew. Residents have decorated it with American flags, roses, carnations, candles, balloons, and wreaths of red, white and blue, and two shiny silver bulletin boards for letters of condolences, expressions of grief.

Children have left pictures drawn in crayon. One child drew stars over water and wrote down two dates: Feb. 1 and Sept. 11.

Here in the debris field, there is much that evokes memories of 9-11, America's last great trauma. Some of the flags are the kind people used to fly from their car windows. The flowers, balloons and candles speak the language of patriotism: United We Stand. Proud To Be An American. Freedom . . . The last best hope upon Earth.

"I feel this just as deeply as 9-11," said Marty Cravy, a 32-year-old Lufkin homemaker. "It's not just seven lives. It's the whole space exploration."

Some residents feel the Columbia tragedy a week ago has affected their community even more strongly than the terrorist attacks on New York City and Washington.

"Just that they found most of the body parts around our little town makes it even more emotional -- a lot more emotional," said Sharon Lambert, 41, of Hemphill, who brought her 3-year-old grandson to visit the memorial.

But that intense, personal feeling of tragedy doesn't seem to extend far beyond the communities where the shuttle rained down in pieces large and small.

Vanessa Elliott, a 30-year-old grocery cashier, said she was appalled when she took her 5-year-old daughter to dance lessons 30 miles from Hemphill to find everybody there was acting as if nothing horrific had happened: "They weren't even talking about it. Totally different than here."

For much of the nation, it is different. There was the initial shock, the disbelief that it had happened again, the wave of sadness for the deaths of the seven astronauts. But now it's back to dance lessons, soccer games, yard work and art festivals -- normal life.

On seeing the shuttle split apart on their television screens, many Americans wondered whether this could be a terrorist act aimed at another symbol of national pride, this one with an Israeli astronaut aboard. When Columbia's loss was downgraded to a colossal accident, the grief remained, but without the fear.

"It was a relief in some ways," said Lisa Sepulvano, 45, of Hemphill. "It would have been a big thing for them to get our shuttle. I did think about that."

This is the mark that Sept. 11, 2001 has left on the American psyche. Seventeen years apart, the nation had two shuttle disasters — Challenger and Columbia. But what happened 17 months ago changed how we measure them.

"The difference between now and when the Challenger blew up is as soon as we heard what happened we asked ourselves, `Was it a terrorist attack?' " said Robert Butterworth, a psychologist with International Trauma Associates in Los Angeles. "It's a different mode of thinking."

Our psychic landscape also reflects the physical characteristics of the disaster.

The attacks that brought down the World Trade Center happened in the most densely populated part of the largest city in the United States. Our emotions after that tragedy were equally intense, condensed and concentrated.

Columbia disintegrated over a much less populated area of the country, a place so lacking a concentration of people that the thousands upon thousands of pieces of debris fell to Earth without hitting a single person.

Pieces of wing, rockets, windows, landing gear, instrument panels, fuselage and insulation tiles are scattered across a dozen counties, hundreds of square miles, and maybe as many as four states. This ground zero is 350 miles long.

Our feelings about this tragedy are similarly scattered and diffused. There are those who are deeply grieving. Those who are still saddened. And those who moved on a day after it happened.

On Tuesday, President Bush gave eloquent testimony to the bravery and sacrifice of the Columbia crew during a memorial service in Houston.

"We find the best among us, send them forth into unmapped darkness and pray they will return," Bush said. "They go in peace for all mankind, and all mankind is in their debt."

But on Wednesday, the focus was back on Iraq as Secretary of State Colin Powell presented the U.S. case to the United Nations. The thoughts of war that Columbia had pushed to the recesses of our minds jerked back to clarity.

On Thursday, NASA Administrator Sean O'Keefe and Vice President Dick Cheney gave their eulogies for the shuttle crew at a moving memorial in Washington.

Then on Friday, while space workers mourned at the shuttle landing strip, the president raised the risk of terrorist attacks to a high alert. The emotional whipsaw of war and tragedy -- the deaths of seven astronauts and the prospect of more Americans sacrificing their lives for their country -- makes it hard to focus.

There's too much to fear, too much to feel, too much to think about. "You can wring only so much emotion from our psyche," said Butterworth, the Los Angeles psychologist. "Sure, we're sad, but we only have so many emotions to give."

If the nation as a whole seems distanced from the Columbia tragedy, there is no such luxury in east Texas, where residents of these small towns still feel the anguish of what happened eight days ago.

They felt it from the moment the first thunderous boom caught them between bites of breakfast or awoke them from their beds. They felt their houses shake and their windows rattle. They heard the long, loud rumble made by large chunks of the space shuttle hurtling through the atmosphere.

Some thought a propane truck had exploded or a gas line erupted. A few of the truly devout thought Judgment Day had arrived. Sabine County Clerk Janice McDaniel thought Hemphill had been bombed.

In a way, it was. Hemphill and Nacogdoches and Palestine

and Bronson and Pineland were bombarded by toxic fragments that smell like ammonia, fish and bleach; charred chunks of tile; sharp metal shards; bits of insulation; pieces of people.

Everyone knows someone who found something on their land. They can't drive to visit friends or shop in Lufkin without passing yellow crime tape or little flags on metal stakes or a bouquet of flowers at the side of the road marking where some piece of the shuttle landed.

Everyone knows someone who is out searching for the debris or baking cakes or frying chicken or making tater-tot casseroles for the men and women who endure the cold and the rain, the briers and thickets, in the drive to retrieve what might be the one piece that solves the puzzle.

"The heart just reaches out and wants to help," said Tammy Tatum, 44, a restaurant owner from Pineland fixing grub for the searchers at VFW Post 10351.

Columbia's wreckage might have landed anywhere, but much of it ended up here where people call themselves country folk and hillbillies. It landed in a place where people are accustomed to volunteering, to acting without being asked. Sabine County has 10,000 people, no town with more than 1,100 residents, and no fire departments that aren't made up of volunteers.

East Texans feel the intensity of the tragedy for all of us who are too far from the disaster, too distracted, too scarred from worse things that have happened. They've given over their towns, businesses, homes and lives to the search.

At Abbott's Barber and Hair Styling Shop, where the dirt parking lot hosts press briefings, there's a water-stained cardboard note tacked to the wood paneling with a hand-lettered quote: "The human heart feels things the eyes cannot see and knows what the mind cannot understand."

In this tragedy, East Texans and those closest to the Columbia astronauts are the heart of the nation.

February 9, 2003

Kimberly Mays: The Baby Switched at Birth

SARASOTA -- Kimberly Mays is the reluctant center of attention in the courtroom, bent intently over a yellow note pad while the parade of psychologists and counselors publicly dissect her psyche.

They reveal her secrets, her dreams, her "night terrors" and her fears. Kimberly has an attention deficiency disorder and mediocre grades in school. Kimberly is "needle phobic." Kimberly is insecure. Kimberly has an identity crisis. Kimberly suffers from "developmental blockage" and is experiencing a strong "adjustment reaction."

Friday, it was Sarasota psychologist Lawrence Ritt - the sixth expert on 14-year-old Kimberly Mays' mental landscape - to testify in the past five days. On Monday, it will be court-appointed psychologist Herbert Goldstein.

The psychology of Kimberly Mays is the centerpiece in the legal turf war between her biological parents - Ernest and Regina Twigg - and her "psychological parent" Robert Mays.

Kimberly has asked Circuit Judge Stephen Dakan to sever the Twiggs' parental claims to her; the Twiggs want the right to visit the daughter they barely know.

Being tugged one way by the Twiggs and the other way by her emotional attachment to Mays, has created hellish "night terrors" for Kimberly, Ritt said. She told him about dreams of living in a glass house with exploding windows that cut and maim her and her father. The meanings of her dreams are clear, Ritt said during his six hours of testimony Friday.

"Kim was feeling she was going to lose it all - her psychological parent, her father. She was very fearful her father was going to be destroyed," Ritt said.

The teenager already has lost a normal childhood. Switched at birth in an unexplained way at a Wauchula hospital, Kimberly went home with Bob Mays and his first wife, Barbara. The Twiggs left with the sickly child they named Arlena, who died of a heart defect at age 9, soon after the Twiggs learned she was not their biological daughter.

In the courtroom, Kimberly seems not to listen to all the things she has heard so many times during the past five years. She mostly doodles, this tall, slender girl with the long neck, wide smile and sad eyes.

She seems to have given up hope of ever living in obscurity again. She enters and leaves the Sarasota County Courthouse every day in a crowd, microphones hanging over her head like cranes, cameramen backpedaling.

Once she wanted to be a movie star; now, she wants to be unknown.

The world already knows more than she wants it to know. It knows she almost failed third grade, she sometimes lies, her best friend's name is Lisa. It knows a $6 million settlement with the Hardy County hospital that mixed up the Twigg and Mays babies has made her a millionaire, but no less unhappy.

To be normal - not exceptional, not extraordinary - is her biggest wish.

She wants the psychologists to stop prying off the top of her head and digging around inside her psyche. She wants the lawyers to stop making her cry. She wants the Twiggs and the reporters to go away.

And she wants the world to stop looking over her shoulder at her drawing of the red flower on the yellow note pad.

August 7, 1993

Georgia Cremation Scandal

NOBLE, Ga. -- They came bearing oak boxes, polished cherry-wood boxes, gold-painted boxes, flower-print boxes, black plastic containers, silver and bronze urns, brown-paper sacks and black plastic bags. They took them down from fireplace mantles, curio cabinets, living-room end tables and family-room shelves and drove to the one-story, red-brick Walker County Civic Center in cars and trucks bearing the plates of Georgia, Tennessee and Alabama.

They carried them with care, holding the containers in both hands as if something precious were inside. They came -- a day-long procession of widows, parents, sons and daughters -- to find out whether the contents were the ashes of their loved ones, or just dirt, stones, dust and cement.

Georgia investigators on Tuesday continued to search Tri-State Crematory here, where scores of discarded bodies that should have been cremated were found strewn about the woods and stacked inside storage sheds. The body count stood at 191, of which 29 had been identified. Investigators also found a casket filled with human remains at the home of the crematory's owner, Ray Brent Marsh, 28. They brought in a backhoe to start digging through mounds of dirt in his backyard that they fear might conceal more bodies. They also were testing a lake behind the crematory's 16-acre property for contamination from human remains.

The horrific scene, discovered Saturday, shocked families.

"You give them your loved one, and you come to find out they gave you back powdered cement," said Rusty Cash, 31, a truck driver for a Chattanooga, Tenn., cement company.

Cash's mother-in-law was among the bodies found on the crematory property. Norma Hutton died Dec. 31 at the age of 55. Cash and his wife kept Hutton's oak box on an end table in their family room, beside an identical box with what the couple hope are the ashes of the dead woman's husband, who died in 1993.

Marsh remained in jail Tuesday on 16 counts of theft by deception. He is being charged with consumer fraud because Georgia does not have a law against defiling corpses -- something the state's lawmakers plan to change in the legislative session that just began.

In the meantime, anxious, grieving family members are being told that it will take days before they know whether the remains they are bringing to the civic center are the ashes of human beings or the stuff used to make patios.

One family member was told that the container held human ashes, but not that of the loved one, whose body was found on the Marsh property. DNA testing, which could take a week or more, is required to determine the identity of the cremains in the urns, and containers.

After Beverly Crawford's husband, Robert Howard Crawford Jr., died at 50 on Feb. 26, she spread some of his ashes on Marco Island, along the site of the Trail of Tears motorcycle rally, and some on the 11th hole of his favorite Chattanooga golf course. Six of his golfing buddies got together, and wherever the best shot landed on the 11th hole, that's where they each tossed a fistful of Crawford's ashes -- if they were really him.

"At least that's where we think he is," said Beverly Crawford, 52, who was told ashes in the cherry-wood box were human cremains. "I don't know if it's him or not. There's always that doubt."

The Crawfords' 18-year-old son is going to provide a DNA sample to help verify the identity of the remaining ashes, but even if the contents in the box prove to be Bob Crawford, his widow said it will never be the same.

"I will put him back in the curio cabinet at home, but I won't talk to him anymore," she said. "I don't feel like it's him."

Michelle Fields risked losing her job in a Cleveland, Tenn., bakery to drive to the crematory to show recovery workers a picture of her sister, Samantha Webb Swinney, who died at 20 on Aug. 31, 2000, of cystic fibrosis.

Fields took time off to drive to St. Petersburg for a one-hour boat ride in the Gulf of Mexico in search of dolphins. On a dreary, gray day, she scattered her sister's ashes among the mammals the woman so loved.

Now Fields has doubts whether her sister's ashes were inside the box.

"I have no way to know if those were her ashes. She might still be out there" on the Marsh property, said Fields, 34.

Her employer gave Fields three days off when Swinney died, but said this time off would go against her. "They said they couldn't give me funeral leave twice for the same person."

Some of those facing the agony of reliving a relative's death and the agony of now knowing the true contents inside the containers were friends of the Marsh family that started the crematory in 1982.

One woman, who was having her husband's ashes tested, said her husband often repaired machinery for Brent Marsh's father, Ray Marsh.

"My husband was good friends with him. We fished on his farm," said the woman, who would not give her name.

Another friend of the Marsh family, retired doctor Garland Kinard, brought a black plastic container for testing with the ashes of his friend's mother, Evelyn Hughes. Kinard said the Marshes where good friends of his and had offered to cremate him at half-price.

"They sat at my table many times," said Kinard, 71. "It's a big surprise. It's just unprecedented."

The wooden boxes and metal urns being carried into the civic center may contain the cremains of friends, lovers and family members, or the ashes of someone unknown, or the stuff of some horrific scam.

But the people bearing those containers carry with them something else -- disbelief, anger and outrage.

"It's kind of harsh, but I'd like to see him cremated alive," said Chris Vandergriff, 31, of Chattanooga, whose mother died of cancer in 1993. "There's no punishment to fit a crime like this."

The people bearing the pain and the boxes say they feel as if they have entered a real-life horror film.

"This is something that happened in the woods, in the backwoods of Georgia," said Ronal D. Akers Jr., 55, whose 34-year-old son was sent to Tri-State for cremation in November.

"These people do not have the same ethical and moral standards that the rest of us do."

Ruby Thomas, 54, said it took her years to recover from the death of her "baby brother," William Richard Mason, who died eight years ago at the age of 36.

Clutching the gold box that once contained what she thought were his cremains, Thomas said she didn't think she would ever recover from the nightmare that started with the gruesome discovery of unburied bodies behind the crematory Saturday.

"I don't think I will ever have peace of mind," said Thomas of Cleveland, Tenn. "It's like a bad dream, like I'm living in a dream and trying to wake up, but I can't."

Seeking peace through prayer, about 100 family members and friends attended a candlelight service Tuesday night at the nearby Oakwood Baptist Church.

"Our heart hurts with your heart," Pastor Darrell Henry said. "We can only say we wish it had never happened to you, and we wish it had never happened to hundreds of others."

February 20, 2002

Anatomy Of An Accident: Six Lives Collide

The sound of the crash was like heavy metal doors slamming shut on the pre-dawn stillness. BANG! . . . BANG! . . . BANG! And then the morning silence returned. Within that flash of time on a two-lane Osceola County road, the destinies of six people collided with a force that still reverberates more than three years later.

Three died. Three emerged scarred forever. In the memories of the survivors and the grief of the families, the accident on Poinciana Boulevard just after 6 a.m. on April 7, 2002, was the beginning of a day that never ended.

The deaths were recorded in snippets of television and a few paragraphs in the newspaper. After the accident, the Orlando Sentinel headline on Page B3 read: "Crash near Poinciana High kills 3."

This is the story of one accident worth telling not because it is more significant than any other. But by considering the causes and consequences of one fatal crash, then multiplying its power and tragedy by all the others like it, we can begin to comprehend the true human toll of the carnage on our roads.

The accident would take the lives of two young men returning from a party. It would kill a middle-aged woman on her way to work at a hotel and cripple her boyfriend. It would haunt a theme-park ride attendant who now takes a bus to his job in Kansas City. It would prove to a woman working at Wal-Mart the power of guardian angels.

The 1999 Chrysler Concorde LXI was flying down Poinciana Boulevard at 70 to 90 mph -- far above the speed limit of 55 mph on the straight stretch of road in front of Poinciana High School.

It was a few minutes before dawn on the first day of daylight-saving time. As the car sped through the darkness, streetlights gleamed off its shiny, black surface.

The tragedy about to unfold started with the poor choices of two young men leaving an all-night party. They were drunk, high and tired when they poured themselves into the car for a six-mile ride home that should have taken less than 15 minutes.

Their bad decisions would soon end their lives and radiate loss and pain into the worlds of people they had never met.

Behind the wheel was Tommy Allen, 20. In the passenger seat was his sister's boyfriend, 17-year-old Brian Smith. Neither was wearing a seat belt. Tommy's bloodstream was a pharmaceutical sewer of painkillers, barbiturates, antibiotics and tranquilizers. He had enough alcohol in his blood to make two people drunk.

Brian had less to drink, but his head still buzzed from painkillers and the street drug Ecstasy. When Brian slipped into the passenger seat of Tommy's car, a friend at the party tried to persuade him not to go. What was the rush? Brian could crash at the party house or sleep it off at his girlfriend's home just down the street.

Besides, Tommy was in no shape to drive. The combination of alcohol and pain pills alone was enough to cause him to pass out. But Brian shook off his friend, determined to get home. Brian didn't like to sleep at other people's houses. Even as a teenager, Brian still wet the bed.

When Brian was about 9, he'd had an operation to cure the problem. But it didn't work. The doctors said he would grow out of it. But he never did. One of Brian's biggest fears at 17 was soiling someone else's sheets. It was a secret shame he shared only with his parents.

But to his friends and classmates, Brian was the flirtatious, fun-loving guy whose personality helped compensate for being the shortest kid in his class. Even now, he stood only 5 feet 5. Girls were drawn to Brian with his blond hair, gray eyes and easy charm. For about a year, Brian had been dating Tommy Allen's younger sister, Jennifer.

Jennifer would write Brian 58 love letters on lined notebook paper, addressed to Bri-Bri and signed Jenny Pooh, which he saved in a plain blue three-ring binder. She wrote him while she was bored in math class, bored in science class, bored in Spanish class. She complained about another girl calling him at home.

Beneath the boy with the goofy grin, there was a kid in trouble. His parents' divorce when he was 15 had set Brian adrift. He had been expelled from school for skipping classes and disciplinary problems, and had been arrested for possession of marijuana.

Even though his father had custody, Brian remained close to his mother. Before the divorce, he had been his mommy's boy. He called her "Mama Dukes." She called him "Bri-Bear" and plied her son with teddy bears, even as a teen.

And in that way, Brian Smith was much like Tommy Allen, who remained close to his mother after his parents also divorced when he was 15. As a young man making money selling time shares, Tommy gave his mother extravagant gifts: Ralph Lauren perfume, a Coach handbag, dinner at Wolfgang Puck. In return, his mother co-signed his car loan, putting the registration to his Chrysler Concorde in her name.

Tommy loved the car he was about to destroy. He spent hours on Saturday mornings washing, waxing, scrubbing and polishing. His back seat was as clean and orderly as his bedroom, where his shirts were always on hangers, his socks and underwear tucked in drawers.

Tommy Allen was the oldest of three children. He was his sister's protector and his brother's role model. But there was also a recklessness to Tommy: He collected traffic tickets like they were baseball cards.

There were other problems, too. The police picked him up once when he and a couple of friends bolted from a Denny's without paying a $33 tab. He was arrested again when they stopped his car in February 2002 and he gave them a fake name -- the name of a friend who was wanted on two warrants.

On the morning of the crash, Tommy was only a mile, just moments, from Brian Smith's house when they passed Poinciana High School, heading south. The speeding Chrysler crossed the yellow line and then jerked back into its own lane.

Two cars and a pickup were rounding the curve by Reedy Creek Elementary School heading north toward the high school. They came closer, and closer still. Then Tommy's car swerved into their lane again.

BANG! Tommy's car grazed the first car, a 1989 Honda Prelude, behind the driver's door. The force spun the blue Honda like a roulette wheel until it stopped in the middle of the road, facing east toward the barbed-wire fences of a cow pasture.

The air bags inside Tommy's car inflated as it glanced off the Honda and shot toward the second northbound car, a 2002 Dodge Dakota pickup.

BANG! The Chrysler hit the pickup head-on. The force of the collision pushed the Dodge backward and flipped it over. The truck landed on its wheels on the side of the road.

Tommy's shiny black car was now airborne, turning counterclockwise directly into the path of the third car, a 1985 Oldsmobile Delta 88.

BANG! The Olds smashed broadside into the passenger side of Tommy's car where Brian Smith was sitting. The final crash stopped the Olds dead in the road, but it bounced Tommy's car backward 24 feet.

In the silence that followed the crash, the Chrysler began to burn.

"There's somebody in there!" shouted a woman, standing beside her van. "Somebody get them out."

A Disney World bus driver and a security guard at Disney's Animal Kingdom ran to the car. The impact had shoved the engine of the Chrysler into the front seat of the car. The front seats had collapsed backward, and Tommy Allen and Brian Smith were lying backward, as if on a bed.

The two men ripped open the driver's door of the burning car and pulled Tommy Allen out. There were air bubbles coming through the blood of his nose.

"This one's alive!" somebody yelled.

But by the time the paramedics reached Tommy's body, it was too late. The air bubbles in the blood, the movements of his body, had been the convulsions of death.

The two men then went to the passenger side of the car. Brian Smith's door was crumpled from being hit by the Oldsmobile, and they had to rip off the frame of the window to pull him out of the car. They laid him on the grass on the side of the road. He died with a look of shock on his face.

Inside the blue Honda Prelude, a Universal Studios ride attendant was struggling to get out.

August 21, 2005

Inside Car 2

With the headlights of Tommy Allen's Chrysler Concorde shining in his windshield, David Reffitt jerked the wheel of his Honda to the right. He felt the passenger-side wheels touch the gravel on the shoulder. They missed me, he thought. But as the words were forming inside his head, the shiny black Chrysler clipped his 1989 Honda Prelude behind the driver's door.

BANG!

It was just a few minutes after 6 a.m. on April 7, 2002. Reffitt was inside his car, yanking at the door jammed shut by the collision.

A month earlier, Reffitt and his wife, Joni, had moved from Kansas City, Mo., to an RV campground outside of Kissimmee. They were trying to settle down, start over, repair their spur-of-the moment marriage. Reffitt was 34. Joni was 47.

Reffitt had always lived an unscripted life: Have fun, enjoy yourself. Reality is what happens between Star Trek and Dungeons and Dragons.

His favorite holiday was Halloween, and every day was Halloween at his new job with Universal Studios, where he dressed like a Canadian Mountie at Dudley Do-Right's Ripsaw Falls flume ride.

On that Sunday morning, his wife was still in bed when Reffitt climbed into his car, fastened his seat belt and left for work with his garage-sale travel mug full of coffee.

Pulling out of the Merry D Campground, Reffitt headed south on Pleasant Hill Road to Poinciana Boulevard. At the traffic light on Pleasant Hill, he turned on Poinciana Boulevard. In his rearview mirror, he could see the headlights of two vehicles.

Reffitt liked the drive up Poinciana Boulevard, a two-lane road with a little wiggle to it that took him past a wildlife preserve, riding stables and pastureland. Despite the new subdivisions sprouting from cow pastures, Poinciana still looked a little like the rural road it used to be.

But residents who live along the road call it a deathtrap. Since 1998, 23 lives have been lost on Poinciana Boulevard -- a ribbon of asphalt built in the early 1980s. At the time, the road served about 3,500 residents. Today, it's the conduit for more than 30,000.

For the tourism-economy workers who live in the ever-expanding subdivisions, the narrow, overworked stretch of roadway is the only way to the attractions and the only way home.

Heading to his job at Universal Studios in the pre-dawn darkness, David Reffitt was listening to a cassette of Mannheim Steamroller's Fresh Aire VI album playing in the tape deck.

There was a chill in the darkness before dawn. A slight fog clung to the pastureland along the road. The moon was a sliver in the sky. The road alternated between darkness and patches of streetlight.

No cars were ahead of Reffitt as he listened to the tape. He sipped from the travel mug and thought he might have enough time to stop for a restroom break and coffee refill.

Reffitt's car cleared the curve by Reedy Creek Elementary School and was headed toward Poinciana High School. Ahead of him, he saw the headlights of Tommy Allen's black Chrysler cross the double yellow lines, as if trying to avoid hitting something in the road, before going back into the southbound lane.

And then, just before the two cars passed each other, the car veered again -- this time coming straight at David Reffitt. The glancing blow from Tommy's Chrysler creased the left side of Reffitt's car. Desperate, he crawled through the shattered driver's window, stunned and in shock.

But no bones were broken. No flesh was cut. Reffitt pulled out his cell phone and called his mother.

The phone rang in Tonya Jo Reffitt's bedroom in Edgewater as she was getting ready for work as a telemarketer.

She heard the voice of her oldest son, but he sounded unfamiliar.

"I believe I was in an accident," he said.

"David?"

"Yeah, I believe I was in an accident, and there is a car on fire, and I believe somebody is dead," Reffitt said.

"Are you OK?" his mother asked.

"I don't know."

Inside Car 3

In the blue pickup behind David Reffitt's car, Bruce Wilson was riding to work beside the woman who had given his life meaning. Geraldine Whitney was what Wilson found when he stopped looking for happiness at the bottom of a bottle. For the first time in his life, he had a purpose beyond the next six-pack.

Wilson knows what it is like to drive drunk. When he was young, he was a lot like Tommy Allen and Brian Smith, who were high on pills and alcohol when their car triggered the fatal four-car crash on Poinciana Boulevard. Bruce Wilson started drinking at 17. He was arrested four times for drunken driving.

In 11th grade, he left school. His adult life was spent tending bar at motorcycle hangouts, working construction and drinking. Mostly drinking.

But by the time of the accident, Wilson had been sober and attending Alcoholics Anonymous for more than two years. He had salvaged his life from alcoholism and despair just in time to find love and happiness. He had a woman, Geraldine, with whom he shared a house, a life, a future.

Geraldine Whitney had her own hard life. She was raised poor, never made it past the eighth grade and married for the first time as a teenager.

As an adult, work was the way Geraldine earned what she never had as a child. She filled her house with collections of unicorns, fairies and angels.

She started calling herself Jerri, and it fit her personality -- a little dynamo of a woman who liked orchestrating parties for family members and co-workers. She had two sons and was married to her second husband for 28 years. A year after he died of a heart attack, Geraldine met Wilson at the Holiday Inn where she was cleaning rooms and he was fixing toilets.

She asked him to help break into her car after she locked her keys inside. The coat-hanger method failed, but a relationship began between the maid and the handyman.

She was 53. He was 45.

Whitney and Wilson didn't talk about marriage, but since moving in together, they had become a team as much as a couple. They worked together at the Quality Inn Maingate West, where Whitney was supervisor of housekeeping and Wilson was a maintenance man whose specialty was patching holes in walls.

Together, they picked out the blue 2002 Dodge Dakota truck, trading in her old minivan for an early Christmas present. The day of the accident, it still had that new-car smell.

Geraldine Whitney awoke early that day from a restless sleep before the alarm clock went off. The night before, she had learned that her stepdaughter from a previous marriage had died suddenly.

As they got ready for work, Wilson suggested that she might want to take the day off.

"Call work, tell them you're not feeling well," he told her.

"And do what -- mope around the house all day?" she replied.

"I'll call in, too," Wilson said. "We'll take the day off together."

"No," she said, "I'll feel better keeping busy."

Bruce Wilson pulled on his white, short-sleeve work shirt with the silver magnetic nameplate above his right pocket. He strapped his Timex watch with the square face to his left wrist and clipped his Leatherman tool to his belt.

Into one pocket of his shorts, he shoveled all his spare change. In the other, he dropped two brass A.A. coins, one for each year of sobriety, and a small silver cross with "Do It" stamped into the metal.

Geraldine Whitney dressed herself in red. Red top. Red shorts. She combed her short blond hair but didn't bother with makeup. For breakfast, she had a cup of black coffee and a

Marlboro cigarette.

Whitney got behind the wheel of the blue pickup. Wilson, with his 7-Eleven travel mug of coffee, slipped in beside her. Before she backed out of the driveway, seat belts had to be buckled. It was her rule.

At the intersection of Pleasant Hill Road and Poinciana Boulevard, Whitney turned left behind David Reffitt's Honda Prelude.

It was a Sunday like every other Sunday. Another workday. Whitney was in no hurry. She liked to get to work early, and they were ahead of schedule when their pickup, heading north, rounded the curve by the elementary school.

BANG!

The head-on impact with Tommy's Chrysler propelled the pickup backward, flipping it once before it came to rest on the east side of the road 57 feet away. The truck landed on its wheels, facing south. The engine and the left front wheel were pushed into the front seat of the car. The frame beneath the seats snapped.

When Wilson regained consciousness, his blood had left a big red stain on the airbag. His watch was broken, the hands stopped at 6:07 a.m. Wilson looked over at his girlfriend, who was leaning forward on the steering wheel.

"Jerri," he said. "Wake up. We need to get out of here."

He unfastened his seat belt and, with the blade on his Leatherman tool, tried to cut the belt loose from Geraldine. But before he could free her, paramedics were there. One of them went over to the driver's side and checked on Whitney.

"Let her go. She's gone," he said.

Others helped Wilson from the car. He tried to stand, but his broken left leg buckled. His right wrist was snapped. His face was as fractured as a jigsaw puzzle. They carried him on a stretcher to the medical-evacuation helicopter and headed to the trauma center at Orlando Regional Medical Center in Orlando.

On Poinciana Boulevard, Wilson and Whitney sometimes found themselves backed up in traffic as a medical-evacuation helicopter airlifted someone injured in a car accident.

And now it was Bruce Wilson inside the helicopter, rising through the air, high above the flashing lights of fire engines, patrol cars and ambulances, and the body of Geraldine Whitney still pinned inside the wrecked blue pickup.

Inside Car 4

Dorothy Aron had the radio in her '85 Olds tuned to an oldies station as she rounded the curve on Poinciana Boulevard, headed to her greeter's job at Wal-Mart. Following close behind, in his 2000 Chevy pickup, was Albert Aron -- her guardian angel.

Since their wedding in 1962 -- when Dot was 18 and Al was 19 -- Albert Aron devoted himself to Dorothy's safety. She wore angel pins on her blue vest, but it was Al who was always there, hovering, watching, trying to protect her.

And nothing scared the guardian angel like the way people drive on Poinciana Boulevard. They speed. They pass on curves. They run you off the road.

So on most days, Albert and Dorothy rode to work together. He would drop her off at the Wal-Mart in Kissimmee where Dot had worked as a greeter since they moved from New Jersey in 1997. And he would pick her up after getting off work at his job as a houseman at Disney's Beach Club and Yacht Club resorts.

But when Albert worked overtime, as he did the day of the crash, Dorothy would drive her 1985 Oldsmobile Delta 88, and Albert would follow in his silver pickup.

The Oldsmobile was long and white with a maroon top and enough room in the back seat for a picnic. It was far more car than Dot needed. But Al had insisted. She needed a car with heft, he told her -- a solid, American-made car.

That Sunday, Dot Aron slipped behind the wheel of the Oldsmobile shortly before 6 a.m. She draped over the front seat her Wal-Mart vest that gleamed with a half-dozen angel pins and then fastened her seat belt.

As she pulled out of the driveway and down the street, Al was behind her in his pickup.

At the intersection of Pleasant Hill Road and

Poinciana Boulevard, Dorothy and Al waited at the traffic light while David Reffitt's Honda Prelude turned right on Poinciana. As the lanes merged, Dot's car slipped in behind Geraldine Whitney's Dodge Dakota.

Al Aron's pickup had just rounded the curve by Reedy Creek Elementary School when the line of vehicles ahead of him collided with the oncoming car containing Tommy Allen and Brian Smith.

Trailing his wife, Albert watched the accident unfold. He saw the black Chrysler clipping the Honda, slamming into the Dodge pickup and then sliding sideways into Dorothy Aron's Oldsmobile.

And he heard the brutal, violent impacts of the crashes on that dark, still Sunday morning: BANG! . . . BANG! . . . BANG!

Albert pulled his truck off to the side of the road. He ran to the Oldsmobile with its front hood pushed up like a tent. He found Dot sitting in the driver's seat, staring straight ahead.

There was blood in her mouth and running down the side of her face from the gash where the roof of the car cut her above the right eye. Her glasses had flown off her face and were wedged between the broken windshield and the crumpled dash. Parts of her dashboard instruments were in the back seat.

"Dot! Dot!" he cried, tugging open her jammed car door.

He unfastened his wife's seat belt and told her he loved her.

Then he ran to the black Chrysler.

"Is everybody OK? Can anybody hear me?" Al Aron said, but no one answered.

And then he saw the flames, little flickers of fire beneath the engine and the rear of the Chrysler.

Running back to his wife, Al Aron asked the other motorists, "Does anybody have a fire extinguisher? Does anybody have a cell phone to call the police?"

Helping Dorothy from the Olds, Al put his arms around his wife and guided her to his Chevy pickup.

"I'm taking my wife to the hospital," he told the others.

Inside her husband's truck, tearing up Poinciana Boulevard toward the hospital, Dorothy Aron was afraid her husband was going to die. Albert Aron kept clutching his chest, where just a few months before he had undergone quadruple-bypass heart surgery. Dot reached over and took his hand.

"Don't worry," she said. "I'm all right."

At Osceola Regional Medical Center, it took 20 stitches to close the gash above Dot's right eye. The stitches bisected her eyelid and extended through her eyebrow. The scar left the eyebrow arched instead of straight, giving her face the look of a perpetual skeptic.

August 22, 2005

After the accident:
MORGUES AND MOURNING

The death of a child delivers grief in different ways.

The violent traffic accident on an ordinary Sunday morning changed everything forever for the parents of Brian Smith and Tommy Allen. Three years later, they have found their own ways to live with the loss of their sons.

Brian's dad: At peace

An hour after the accident on April 7, 2002, Steve Smith awoke feeling something was wrong. His son was not home from the party, but that was not unusual. Sometimes Brian came home at 8 or 9 in the morning.

On this morning, Brian's absence came with a soundtrack: the sirens on Poinciana Boulevard.

When Smith and his girlfriend left to go fishing that day, they turned north on Poinciana and were blocked by police officers, firetrucks and flashing lights. Smith stopped his car, got out and started walking toward the wreckage of a burned car in the middle of the road. He could see a body on the ground, covered by a blue sheet.

It was Brian beneath the blue sheet. But an Osceola

County deputy sheriff turned him away, and Smith left the scene without finding out for sure whether it was his son on the side of the road.

In his gut, he knew. But he didn't want to believe.

Smith lived the rest of the day in denial. He and his girlfriend went fishing. They left a variety box of doughnuts on the kitchen counter for Brian. They went to lunch. They bought office supplies. They went grocery shopping and bought the Teddy Grahams, Hot Pockets and Bagel Bites that Brian liked.

The day in denial ended with a phone call from Smith's ex-wife, Janee. Two Florida Highway Patrol troopers were in her house. And they had bad news.

"It's me," she said. "There's been an accident on Poinciana. Brian's been killed."

Three years later, Smith says he is at peace with the loss of his son, grateful for the time they had to become closer. He likes to remember Brian as he saw him the last day of his life: joking, teasing, goofing, happy.

"If you ever wanted a day, and you have one day with your son, that would be the day," says Smith, 44. "It was like the greatest gift."

The father never visits his son's grave. Instead, Steve Smith stops at the site of the accident. He pulls off on the side of Poinciana Boulevard where three white crosses once stood.

With the engine off, he talks to Brian. He tells his son he misses him. He loves him. He tells Brian he tries to make good choices and asks for his help.

"That burned spot is where I see Brian when I think of a gravesite," Smith says. "It's where I feel his spirit."

Brian's mom: Still grieving

At 10 p.m. on the day Brian died, his mother and sister arrived at the darkened, brown-brick building of the Orange-Osceola Medical Examiner's Office in Orlando. An employee led them down a narrow gray hallway to the viewing room on the second floor. About the size of a clothes closet, the room had a wooden ledge along two walls and a rack with brochures that read, "What Do I Do Now?"

On the other side of a picture window, on a stainless-steel gurney with a sheet pulled up to his chin, lay Janee Smith's youngest child. Behind him, a mauve curtain was drawn to block the view of the room where autopsies are performed.

Smith turned away from the window, took two steps and pounded her fists on the wall.

"Oh God oh God oh God," she wept. She returned to the window and spoke to her son. "Brian, what happened? What did you do, Brian?"

She studied his face. She wanted to reach through the window, touch his face, brush the dirt from his hair.

"Oh, Heather," she said to her daughter, "he has a cut on his lip, and there's dirt in his hair."

That night, she signed the papers identifying the dead boy on the silver tray as her son. She was given a zip-lock bag with all his possessions: a Velcro wallet, a silver-metal necklace, a gold earring and a brass ring from a trip to Tarpon Springs with BRIAN spelled in capital letters.

Janee Smith Lackey, who remarried after her son's death, keeps the plastic baggie from the morgue inside a cardboard box that holds the souvenirs of a life cut short. From birth to death -- 17 years -- it all fits inside an archive box labeled "Xmas presents."

One by one, she pulls out the possessions that were once just the ordinary stuff of a child growing up. Now it's the inventory of what's left to mourn.

Inside a square, little red box are the baby teeth Brian Smith slipped beneath his pillow for the tooth fairy. There's a child's crayon drawing inside a picture frame. There's a pair of green footprints on white paper labeled "Brian's Feet."

The box is a reminder of all that Brian was and all that he will never be.

At 45, Lackey misses her son so much that she has gone to Cassadaga, the community of psychics, to find him. She believes his spirit inhabits her house.

On the shelf of a corner hutch is "Brian's nickel." Lackey was vacuuming the room when the nickel fell off an end table. She put it back on the table, and it jumped off again. In the same room is "Brian's lamp," which she said turns itself on and off when nobody is in the room.

Her personal penitence for her son's death is to relive it every two weeks, talking to victim-awareness classes for men and women arrested for driving while impaired.

Lackey walks into the stark white classroom with pictures of Brian in her arms. Here is Brian at 3. Here is Brian at 16. And then she holds up a framed photograph of his tombstone.

"This is the most recent picture of Brian. It's all I got," she says. "He was my baby. My little boy. When he died, so much died with him. Hope. Future."

The talks do nothing to cure her grief. Friends tell her it's time to move on, get over it. She can't; she won't.

With her magnified sense of loss, Janee Smith Lackey can't stand to hear people complain about the small problems of their lives. All those things other people take so seriously, she finds so insignificant.

She wants to scream at them, "I'll take your scratched car. You give me back my kid."

Tommy's mom: No regrets

Cathy Brady identified Tommy Allen, her 20-year-old son, at the morgue at 11:05 a.m. the morning after his death. Looking through the plate-glass window, she was struck by how much her son looked like her brother David.

His body on the stainless-steel gurney took her back to the girl she was at 15 and her first experience with death.

Sixteen-year-old David Lofquist was in a head-on collision on a slick and snowy road in Upper Michigan. Thrown from the car, he died three days before Christmas. He was buried on Christmas Eve. Cathy and David were as close as Tommy was to his sister Jennifer. Brady knew the grief that her daughter was feeling. And now she knew the grief her mother had felt.

As she looked at her son and saw her brother, Cathy Brady thought of her mother: "My mom had to do this. She's OK.

I'll be OK."

The pattern of Cathy Brady's life has been love and loss. After David's death, she became close to her older brother Bob, who died suddenly in 1996. Five years earlier, her father died of cancer at 57.

Death has taught Brady to live life without regrets. There's no replay button after someone is gone that allows us to go back and say the things that were never spoken, spend time together instead of apart, mend broken fences.

"I got to see him grow to be 20," Brady says. "What haunts you are the things you didn't do that you wish you had done. I have no regrets. Things between us were really good."

There is sadness, but it doesn't come from the missed opportunities of the past or the events that will never happen in the future. The sorrow, when it comes, arrives unannounced while she is barbecuing chicken on the grill. She is baking a pumpkin pie. She is cooking a big meal.

"Even three years later, when something strikes you the right way, it is very sad. When it comes around, it's a lot deeper," says Brady, 41.

It's a profound loneliness she feels in the stomach, deep in the gut. The ache inside, Brady says, feels like she is starving to death.

August 23, 2005

Three years later:
SCARS STILL LINGER

David Reffitt, Dorothy Aron and Bruce Wilson escaped death, but not without injuries and traumas. For the survivors of the tragic accident on April 7, 2002, the scars are both deep and invisible, painful and still healing

David Reffitt: Why did I live?

Of the six people involved in the accident, David Reffitt was the only one to walk away.

He suffered a small cut on his knee, scrapes and bruises on his elbow and wrist. No hospitals, no surgeries, no rehab.

Call him lucky. But nobody escapes unscathed.

His injuries don't show on the outside, but the trauma of that day has never left him. It shows itself in his fear of driving and his search for the meaning of his own survival.

Now 37, Reffitt asks the questions that have no answers. He wonders why others died and he survived.

"I was meant to be in the accident to learn something. Maybe it was that my life was not going the way it was supposed to, and this was a wake-up call: `Hey, dude, you're going the wrong way,' " he says.

After the crash, Reffitt separated from his wife, left his ride-attendant job at Universal Studios, declared bankruptcy and began to drift.

The awful sound of car hitting car, the images of headlights in his windshield, the jolt of impact, revisited Reffitt every time he got behind the wheel after the accident, so he stopped driving.

He went wherever Greyhound would take him. The bus would stop, and he'd step off in some town he had never been in before, some city he had never seen. He'd take a job -- handyman, lawn mowing, convenience-store clerk -- stay awhile and move on.

"It's like he lost something," says his brother Robert, who lives with David in a two-bedroom apartment they share in Kansas City. "He is trying to find something that he is never going to find."

A thousand miles from Poinciana Boulevard, David Reffitt now takes a two-hour bus commute to his job stocking shelves at a Kansas City-area Wal-Mart. He sits at the back of Bus 28 and stares out the window, sometimes seeing the crosses from other accidents that people erect on the side of the road.

To his Wal-Mart co-workers, he is just the guy on the forklift, shuffling around pallets of Kellogg's Limited Edition Star Wars cereal and Sam's Choice soda, working 10 to 6, Sundays and Tuesdays off.

But Reffitt is a living memorial to what happened on Poinciana Boulevard that morning. He was the only one to walk away. And for the rest of his life, he will wonder why.

"I survived that accident for a reason," Reffitt says. "I may never know what that reason is."

Dorothy Aron: The scar

Three years later, the scar arching through her right eyebrow has faded into just another crease on her face. Nobody would know it's there if they didn't know where to look.

"I'm very conscious of it," says Dorothy Aron, now 61. "It doesn't belong there."

She sees it every morning in the mirror. She can't ignore it. It is a permanent reminder of the damage inside. She still has neck and shoulder pain. Sometimes her left arm goes numb and her hand feels cold. There are memory lapses and the big blank space in her mind between the time she left the driveway and the moment she heard her husband yelling, "Dot! Dot!"

To replace the wrecked white-and-maroon Olds, Albert Aron bought Dorothy another car. A bigger car. A safer car. A more substantial car.

He bought her a 1979 Cadillac Eldorado -- an old person's Hummer. But it never felt right. A car that big made Dot Aron, a petite woman, feel even smaller, more vulnerable.

Only once since the accident has Dot driven down Poinciana Boulevard by herself. She did it inside that monstrous Cadillac -- without telling Albert.

She did it in defiance of her fear.

It was about six months after the crash, on a Sunday. Al had to work overtime, and on those days, Dorothy drove the Cadillac to work while Albert followed.

Normally, when she got off work, she would go five miles out of her way to take Pleasant Hill Road home. But on this day, she turned left on Oren Brown Road and drove one mile to Poinciana Boulevard.

She waited at the corner for the cars to pass and then

eased the Cadillac onto Poinciana. It was late afternoon, and the traffic was light. She felt good behind the wheel, regaining confidence with every mile.

But as the car passed Poinciana High School, her arms began to shake. Her whole body started to tremble. As she approached the spot of the accident, she saw the three crosses at the side of the road for the first time.

There was the tall one for Geraldine Whitney that stood back from the road, built by her son from scrap lumber he found in her garage, and covered with the felt-pen prayers of her family. And the smaller crosses for Tommy Allen and Brian Smith, set apart from Whitney's marker and closer to the road.

And then she saw the blackened spot in the road where Tommy's car burned so hot it melted the asphalt.

"My God," she thought, "it could have been me."

She got her courage back that day. But Al -- her guardian angel -- was outraged. It's too dangerous, Albert said. He made her promise never to drive again. And she hasn't. Albert Aron gave up working overtime so that they could ride to work and back together.

These days, Dorothy lives life as a passenger. Al is her taxi service. If Dot needs to get her hair done, Al takes her. If she has a day off, she waits for Al to come home and they run errands together.

When they drive down Poinciana Boulevard, Dorothy Aron still can't avert her eyes from the accident site. The crosses are gone. The only evidence is the spot in the middle of the road where the car burned.

But time, tires and the torrential rains of the hurricanes have rubbed and washed away much of the stain.

"I can't really see that spot," she confesses.

Like the scar on her face, it's noticeable only to those who know where to look.

Geraldine, Bruce: Undying love

The day of Geraldine Whitney's funeral, members of her family posed for a photograph of the white wooden cross they would erect at the site of the accident. There are 36 people in the picture.

Geraldine was the second-youngest of seven children. But she was the glue that held everybody together -- the one who organized reunions, staged birthday parties, orchestrated family events.

When she died, at 53, the family lost its nucleus. Her older sister feels abandoned.

"It's like I'm walking alone in this world," says Lillian Lamb, 63.

She blames her unending unhappiness on the reckless boys who killed Geraldine.

"They were drunk and partying," Lamb says. "The people who did this to her, I hate them."

Geraldine lost her life that day and, although he lived, so did Bruce Wilson. These days, Bruce Wilson sees the world through double vision. The doctors who rebuilt his face were unable to realign his eye sockets, so the right eyeball sees things a little higher than the left. When he touches his left temple, he can feel the screws beneath the skin holding his fractured skull together. There are rods in his left leg and right wrist. All the toes of his left foot are missing.

He has boxes of unpaid medical bills. One hospital bill totaled $344,921.07 -- more than Wilson would make in 19 years as a hotel Mr. Fix-it.

At 49, Wilson's days of Harley-Davidson motorcycles are gone. The days of matching screwdriver to screw are over. The days of running down the street, reading a book, building a birdhouse, patching a hole in the wall, belong to the past.

Doctors reassembled his body, but pieces are missing that can't be replaced. He has learned to walk on the bones of his foot without any toes. And to live with the loss of the woman he loved.

A recovering alcoholic, Wilson has remained sober three years after the accident. He lives now with his elderly parents a mile from Geraldine's grave. When he visits the cemetery, he brings her a red rose picked out for him by his mother.

His candy-red motorized wheelchair has a long, silver flashlight strapped to one side and a can of Fix-A-Flat tucked in the back. Its maximum speed is 2 mph. On his way to her grave, Wilson is passed by kids on skateboards as his electric wheelchair negotiates crosswalks and curb cuts.

At the entrance to the Osceola Memory Gardens Cemetery and Funeral Home, he steers the wheelchair through the rows of grave markers. At an oak surrounded by engraved park benches, he turns right and stops before the bronze marker set into pink granite. Stuck inside the bronze urn are artificial pink roses and baby's breath. No flower arrangement is complete, Geraldine always said, without baby's breath.

Wilson slips the red rose, the real thing, from its clear plastic sleeve. He pushes himself off the seat of the wheelchair and pokes the rose into the center of the arrangement. With his left hand, he brushes a stray twig from the grave marker.

He sits back into the wheelchair. He stares at the grave marker that says, in raised bronze letters, "Geraldine `Jerri' Whitney. October 11, 1948 -- April 7, 2002. Loved and missed by many."

And then he talks to his dead girlfriend. He tells her he loves her, he misses her. He wishes she were here.

"I'm trying the best I can," he says. "I miss you. I wish it didn't happen the way it did."

The sun is starting its slide toward the horizon. Wilson pulls off his cap and wipes a shirt sleeve across his forehead. The shadow from the oak tree reaches across the graves. The tip of the shadow touches the edge of Geraldine's gravestone like a caress.

August 24, 2005

In Living Memory: A Year After 9/11

Let us never forget to remember the day.

The terrorist attacks of Sept. 11, 2001, left a lasting imprint on us all — not as a perfectly preserved photograph framed forever in the brain, but as a day still alive and growing, us, a living memory that changes us even as we change it.

Sept. 11 is a collective memory, something that joins us, unites us, makes us millions of tiny pieces in the same mosaic. But it is also an individual memory, a very personal and particular memory. What we remember, how we remember it and how that memory affects our lives depend on those things that make us individuals — age, knowledge, experience, perspective, fears, hopes and desires.

"Memory is not just a video recording or a photograph. It's a combination of what is already in our memory from past experience and new information coming in," says Harvard psychologist Daniel L. Schacter. "We encode an event differently and remember it differently."

The living memory of Sept. 11 is different for 80-year-old Nancy Hollis Dillard, who turned 20 the day Pearl Harbor was bombed, than it is for 8-year-old Lazaro Dubrocq, who was sitting in the front row of a Sarasota classroom when President George W. Bush learned of the attacks on the World Trade Center.

And the memory is different for Lazaro, who loves animals and remembers that the president said he had two dogs and a cat, than for his second-grade teacher, Kay Daniels, who can't think of the attacks without remembering her father's death the following month.

"They are definitely intertwined," says Daniels, 45. "I think of the families that lost loved ones on Sept. 11, and I feel what they felt."

The horror of that day is preserved on film and newsprint, in poetry, journals and the crayon drawings of schoolchildren. But the living memory of the event lasts only as long as we do. When the last person to remember Sept. 11 dies, so will the dimension that can't be preserved on videotape and paper — the intensely personal, intimate impact of witnessing those cataclysmic events.

The memory will die, and the moment will pass forever into history. It will become something taught, learned and studied by those who weren't there, who didn't share the experience.

We lost our living memory of the Civil War in 1956 when the last veteran died at the age of 112.

The Spanish-American War ended in 1899, but the living memory didn't pass until the last soldier died in 1992 at age 106.

The living memory of the Titanic resides inside three women, the last survivors, all in their late 90s.

Of the 4.73 million Americans who served in World War I, fewer than 550 are left.

Members of the Pearl Harbor Survivors Association are dying at the rate of two a day. The average age of the 7,600 survivors is 83.

A hundred years from now, the last living memory of Sept. 11 may reside inside the centenarian brain of Lazaro Dubrocq or his classmates.

The 16 schoolchildren sat in the front row of history when White House Chief of Staff Andrew Card entered Kay Daniels' room from an adjoining classroom, walked up to the president and whispered into his ear, "A second plane has hit the World Trade Center. America is under attack."

Daniels remembers the moment: "From the look on his face, I knew something had happened. He left me. Mentally, he was not here."

The children in the classroom have different memories of that day. The excitement of the president's visit to their reading class is mixed with the events that cut his visit short. Mariah Williams remembers reading to the president. Tyler Radkey remembers shaking the president's hand. Jamie Jones remembers President Bush gave Mrs. Daniels a hug. Danyelle Green remembers the president had to leave.

Natalia Pinkney recalls, "One plane crashed into the World Trade Center and one into the White House."

Chantal Guerrero recollects, "I was scared because the people were trying to kill the president and the president was with us."

LaDamian Smith remembers, "Thousands of people died."

The Emma E. Booker Elementary schoolchildren have no experience, no memory, with which to compare the terrorism they witnessed that day. But the event immediately triggered a chain reaction of remembrances for 90-year-old Frances Jackson, who was transported in her mind from her eighth-floor apartment in Orlando's Westminster Towers back to the start of World War II and from there to the end of World War I.

"One thing brings you back to something terrible that happened before," she says.

Jackson remembered being at home on Stetson Avenue in College Park with her husband and 22-month-old son on that Sunday afternoon when the radio announced that the Japanese had attacked the American fleet in Pearl Harbor. She remembers thinking, “This means war, another world war,” and that thought brought memories of being 6 years old in rural Virginia when World War I ended.

Robert A. Leonard, a 50-year-old researcher with the federal Department of Housing and Urban Development, stores his memory of Sept. 11 in a locked cabinet inside his mind. What he remembers is driving to work in his 1995 Mazda Protege on Washington's Interstate 395 that Tuesday morning when American Airlines Flight 77 filled his rearview mirror.

On the radio was the news that two jetliners had crashed into the World Trade Center in New York. When Leonard looked again, the plane was in his driver's-side mirror, flying low to the ground. He pulled his car off to the side of the highway and watched as the plane banked and then accelerated as it slammed into the side of the Pentagon.

"It went into the wall of the Pentagon easily, intact. It didn't buckle or anything," he recalls. "There was a pause when the plane was totally absorbed inside the Pentagon. There was this plane-sized hole in the Pentagon. Then there was this fireball shooting into the air about three stories high."

Leonard says he can replay the memory in his head, freezing the images in his mind. But there is no sound on his tape. No sound except for his own screams.

The memory of what he witnessed so traumatized Robert Leonard that he decided after a month to put the images away in a part of his brain where they remain under lock and key. But when he chooses to remember, the images are intact, as real as the day they were burned into his brain.

"It's a film that will always be in that filing cabinet. I can open that drawer and get it out any time," he says. "It has become like the Zapruder film from the Kennedy assassination. It's not a continuous film. It's like individual pictures. I can play it over and see every frame."

Leonard thinks of his memory as an indelible image forever frozen inside his mind. But memory doesn't work that way.

It isn't some time capsule filled with mementos stored inside the back closet of the brain. Our memories are imprecise and incomplete even at the time they are forming. Some Sarasota schoolchildren think they remember what Andrew Card said to President Bush, although none could possibly have heard what he whispered into the president's ear.

Memories — even ones as strong, sharp and shocking as those of Sept. 11 — are not immune to time, imagination, embellishments and media influences.

The elderly survivors of the Titanic remember things that never happened but were erroneously reported or appeared in film versions of the disaster, says Edward Kamuda, founder of the Titanic Historical Society near Springfield, Mass.

"Time has dimmed the minds of all these people. They remember what their mothers or others told them. They've seen the movies. They see all these things, and that clouds their real memories," he says.

Our memories of Sept. 11 are already subjected to the revisions of a brain filled with images from television cameras, tourist camcorders and photographs.

In her mind, Dagmar Santana remembers watching Good Morning America with the volume turned down when the first plane hit the World Trade Center. She insists she saw it live — but the TV broadcast of the attack began after the first plane's impact.

"I saw this building, and I thought, `Wow, that airplane is too close.' Then it crashed into the tower. I turned up the volume. And then the second airplane hit the building," says Santana, a 35-year-old Orlando deli worker.

If the exact details of Sept. 11 are beginning to blur, remembering where we were when the attacks happened is still solidly anchored inside our minds.

Of the weeks stacked upon months piled on years, only a few days stand out where the mind can take us back to the exact time and place we witnessed something as memorable as the terrorist attacks of a year ago.

How many of those "flashbulb" memories we experience depend on how directly the event affects our own lives. Researchers found that both blacks and whites remembered where they were when John F. Kennedy was assassinated.

About half the blacks and whites remembered where they were when Robert F. Kennedy was shot. But 32.5 percent of whites and 75 percent of blacks remembered where they were when the Rev. Martin Luther King Jr. was killed.

Kay Daniels' 80-year-old mother remembers where she was when King was assassinated April 4, 1968. She was alone in her husband's service station in Palmetto when the news came on the radio. She remembers the tears on her cheeks and the sadness in her chest.

"I was like in shock and didn't want to believe it," says Rosa Mae Johnson. "It hurt so bad. It just grieved my heart to lose such a good man."

It's this personal collection of memories — some shared with others, others uniquely our own — that make us individuals. Memory is self. It's who we are.

The mind isn't a computer with unlimited memory. And memory isn't a travelogue of our lives, documenting every experience of every day.

It's more like the composition-book journals that fill three shelves in the den of Nancy Hollis Dillard's Orlando home. Dillard has been keeping journals since 1962, 152 volumes in all.

They aren't diaries that detail her daily routines, but thoughts, feelings, events and memories she felt worth preserving.

If she wants to remember where she was, what she thought, or how she felt when Kennedy was killed or the space shuttle Challenger exploded, Dillard can go back to her journals and retrieve those memories.

But she can't do that for every day of her life. There are gaps where days pass, and nothing is recorded. And there are moments, feelings and memories she decided not to record. There is nothing, for example, in her journals about what she saw as a 24-year-old Army nurse ordered to witness the atrocities of the Buchenwald concentration camp in 1945. It was a memory she chose not to remember until 55 years later, when she felt compelled to write down her remembrances to refute those who claimed the Holocaust never happened.

"There, in front of us on the cold stone floor of a wide courtyard, lay a pile of corpses in a jumble like a cord of stovewood released from the bed of a dump truck," she wrote in 2000.

Writing those words took Nancy Hollis Dillard back in time to something more personally horrifying than watching the death and destruction of Sept. 11 via television.

"It's really bright in my mind — the meeting of the eyes of the dead with the eyes of the living. I can still see it; I can still smell it," Dillard says.

Similarly, Robert Leonard says he needed to hide away the memory of that plane crashing into the Pentagon to avoid losing his mind altogether.

Never a fan of country music, he nonetheless used a country song he associated with a happier time — the marriage of a nephew — to take his mind off the memory. He played the CD with the song — Lee Ann Womack's "I Hope You'll Dance" — while on his way to and from work and whenever he was home alone with his thoughts.

"I played it over and over again," Leonard says. "Since the experience was totally visual, I used music to try and calm myself and get this film put away in the back of my mind."

Memory isn't just about reliving the past — it's the way the brain deals with the present and the future. It's how we learn from experience, adapt and evolve.

So just as the mind changes memory, memory changes us.

Robert Leonard says that after Sept. 11, he found himself compelled to help others — spending time he never thought he had to mentor high-school students, supervise a church youth group and coach his son's basketball team.

For many Americans, the most profound change provoked by the living memory of Sept. 11 is the fundamental way we view the world. We have a different understanding of international terrorism, the Middle East, Islam, the geography and politics of Afghanistan, the conflict between Israelis and Palestinians.

Sept. 11 left many Americans with a feeling of vulnerability and the uneasy sense that we may never be as safe, or as free, as we were before that day.

"I feel we're not protected. We're not safe. You're never safe," says Anthony Farina, a 44-year-old Bithlo pipe fitter.

His 13-year-old daughter, Pricilla, carries with her the living memory of a society transformed by one horrific day in September. She lives in an America that no longer believes such a thing can't happen here, but a nation that presumes it will happen again.

"It's going to happen again, but when we think we're safe," says Pricilla Farina. "It could be two years from now."

A stain on our soul, Sept. 11 is something we can never forget. The living memory of that day is as much a part of us as the living memory of Sept. 11, 1943 is a part of Kenneth F. Peloquin.

For 58 years, the retired Leesburg man didn't let Sept. 11 pass without thinking about the day when an enemy plane dropped a bomb on the USS Savannah off the coast of Italy, killing 206 American sailors and wounding 13, including himself.

The memory of that day, in many ways, defines who Kenneth Peloquin is — the single moment that preserves the 22-year-old sailor inside the 80-year-old man.

For the past 33 years, Peloquin has been attending reunions with a shrinking number of Savannah survivors.

He was on his way to Denver for the annual reunion on Sept. 11, 2001, when his plane was diverted to Atlanta.

Inside the airport, he found the world had changed while he was in midair.

"The place was jammed with people looking at different TVs. Babies were crying. People were knee-deep at the pay telephones. There were people on cell phones. All kinds of noise," he recalls.

The attack on the World Trade Center happened almost to the exact hour 58 years after the bombing of the Savannah — a coincidence that didn't occur to Peloquin until the next day.

"The focus was on what had happened, the buildings coming down. It shook the thoughts of my ship out of my mind," he says.

On Sept. 11, 2001, Kenneth Peloquin forgot to remember.

September 11, 2002

www.ingramcontent.com/pod-product-compliance
Lightning Source LLC
Chambersburg PA
CBHW061432210726
48287CB00007B/2183
* 9 7 8 1 9 4 3 3 0 7 0 3 6 *